DDAY

DATE DUE

NOV 15 1993 OCT 22			
NOV 14 1994 OCT 29 1997			
NOV 21 1994 NOV 2 1997			
NOV 28 1994 OCT 03 2000			
OCT 23 1995 NOV 20 2000			
OCT 31 1995 NOV 16 2002			
NOV 16 1995 NOV 22 2002			
NOV 23 1995 NOV 22 2002			
SEP 29 1997			
OCT 08 1997 NOV 27 2003			
NOV 15 2002			

JOE HOWE

JOE HOWE
The Man Who Was Nova Scotia
by Kay Hill

Joseph Howe (1804-1873) as a young man.

McCLELLAND AND STEWART

The Canadian Publishers,
McClelland and Stewart Limited,
25 Hollinger Road,
Toronto, Ontario.
M4B 3G2

CANADIAN CATALOGUING IN PUBLICATION DATA

Hill, Kay, 1917-
  Joe Howe

Bibliography: p.

ISBN 0-7710-4096-2

1. Howe, Joseph, 1804-1873.   2. Politicians – Nova
Scotia – Biography.

FC2322.1.H68H55   971.6'02'0924   C79-094932-6
F1038.H68H55

Photo credit: All photographs in
this book are used with the kind
permission of the Public Archives
of Nova Scotia.

Printed and bound in Canada
by John Deyell Company

Contents

To Norman Creighton,
hard critic, patient friend

Foreword

"We were the first colony to achieve responsible government, that is, government responsible to the majority in the legislature rather than to an appointed group."

> –from a speech by the Hon. R.L. Stanfield to the Overseas Press Club of America, reported in *My Years with Stanfield*, by E.D. Haliburton, Lancelot Press, Windsor, N.S., 1972.

This is the story of the man who led Nova Scotia in her battle for responsible government, the man who demonstrated for the first time to Britons everywhere how colonists could, lawfully and peacefully, win this measure of democracy.

Wilful, witty, generous and brave, this early Halifax newspaperman challenged power and privilege, made fun of royal governors, and fought a duel in defence of his principles. With glowing words, he laid spells on the sophisticates of London and Detroit as easily as he laid them on the twelve Halifax jurors at his trial for libel. Though often criticized for human failings, he was greatly loved in his lifetime. Today, an annual Joseph Howe Festival helps keep his memory green in Nova Scotia.

Much has been written of Joe Howe, as he always liked to be called, and his own voice may be heard directly in diaries, letters, speeches and state papers. Teachers of both elementary and high school classes, however, asked for more. They said their students needed a full length imaginative portrait of the man, which would entertain even as it instructed. Librarians wanted a popular account of his life which would make responsible government and Confederation a bit easier for their younger patrons to understand. And then there were adults – Nova Scotians who knew Howe only as "the man who kissed every woman in Nova Scotia" and Canadians outside the province who kept asking "But *why* did he fight Confederation?" –

who wanted to learn, not everything perhaps, but something more, about the famous Nova Scotian.

This book was the result.

Ketch Harbour, N.S.,
November 21, 1979

CHAPTER ONE
1804-1814

"He left me nothing but his example."

George Johnson Papers

On a sunny day in the summer of 1811, in Halifax, the small wood-and-cobblestone capital of the British colony of Nova Scotia, a man and a six year-old boy made their way up Spring Garden road to where Pyke's bridge crossed the brook. As they walked, they talked – at least, the boy did. The tall grey-haired man with the Bible under his arm listened and smiled encouragement, until the peace of the day was shattered by angry sounds.

"Oh yus? We'll board Yankee vessels any time we likes." The voice was British and came from a grove of spruce on the far side of the brook.

"Keep it up," a second voice growled, "and you'll get a lesson you British won't never fergit."

"From yer tuppeny navy? Hah! Nobody fools with the British, mate. King George, 'ee rules the sea."

An angry splutter came from beyond the trees. "Us Americans don't give a damn fer kings, old Farmer George in partic'lar. I spit on 'im!"

The boy flushed with anger. The gall of that Yankee, insulting King George in the very streets of the loyal colony of Nova Scotia. Taught to love Britain and the Empire, Joe had no use for those English colonists who, thirty years before, had declared their independence of Great Britain and now called themselves citizens of the United States of America.

"Ho, do ye now?" came a shout of outrage. "Lessee can you fight then, as good's ye spit!"

Joe was at his father's heels as they hurried across the bridge. If there was to be a fight, he wanted to see it, take part in it too if Britain's champion needed aid. Rounding the hedge, they came upon two seamen in canvas breeches, hair tied in pigtails, threatening each other with clenched fists. "Hold on, lads," commanded the boy's father, and the men turned tipsy glares on John Howe. "Brawling in the streets of Halifax is forbidden," Mr. Howe explained gently, "particularly on the Sabbath. Shake hands now, like good fellows."

The American replied with an oath, the Briton with a certain vulgar gesture. Their pugnacity found a new direction.

"'oo's 'ee?" queried the English sailor with scorn.

"Stay out of this, old man," growled the Yankee.

"If I did," John Howe said with a smile, "I should be neglecting my duty as a magistrate."

"Magistrate?" The Britisher had spotted the Bible. "Preacher more like."

"In the States," the American grinned, with meaning, "we eats his sort for breakfast."

With nods of mutual encouragement, the two charged John Howe.

"Hold my Bible, Joseph." Though tall and powerful, Joe's father was nearly sixty, not by nature a fighter, and outnumbered. His son squared up beside him, therefore, ready to use fists and boots wherever he saw a chance. But John Howe was a rock on which the sailors struck without effect. Each man was grasped by the neck, swung back and forth several times and then, as Joe watched in growing admiration, had their heads bumped together. Finally, a thrust of the magistrate's shoulder sent them staggering ten paces in opposite directions before they struck the ground.

"Now, lads," said Joe's father, not even out of breath, "lie still for a bit and when you're sober, go back to your ships. My Bible, Joseph." Peacefully, the two continued their walk,

John Howe Senior (1754-1835) father of Joe Howe.

Joe gazing up at his father's face, love enlarged to hero worship.

"I should have punched them!"

The magistrate gave his son a look of gentle reproach. "Joseph, Joseph, surely you haven't forgotten so soon what the preacher told us this morning?"

Joe tried to remember, but truth to tell, he had not listened very closely to the long Sandemanian sermon. Papa was a Sandemanian, and Sandemanians were dissenters, Christians, that is, who did not belong to the official Anglican church. They hated violence and believed all men should practise brotherly love. Churches and ritual were to them unimportant, even destructive of true piety. The boy took a chance. "Christians should love their enemies."

Papa nodded.

"All of them?" The boy thought of the American seaman and of Papa who, born and bred a citizen of Massachusetts Bay colony, had been obliged to leave his home in Boston in 1776 with little but the clothes on his back. "Even the Americans?"

John Howe smiled. "Even the Americans." The boy was puzzled. Papa was always telling him it was right to defend the weak and oppressed, yet the Sons of Liberty had claimed to be doing that when they fought England to free the colonists from unjust taxation. "Did you think the Stamp Tax was fair, Papa?"

"Not at all." Well, it hadn't been cowardice, Joe knew, that had made his father remain loyal to King George. Young John Howe had been a medical orderly, serving the wounded on both sides, under the very guns of Bunker Hill.

"You wonder why I chose the Loyalist side," his father said, understanding. "I was trying, as any Sandemanian would, Joseph, to keep the peace but patience was also needed. I knew Britain herself suffered from the rule of poor, misguided George the Third and his statesmen. When they were gone, Britain's traditional love of justice would have led her to remove the taxes. After all, what need had we British of new political forms?" John Howe's voice warmed with love and pride. "We were rich in freedom even then, compared to other countries. What other nation had a *Magna Carta*, the charter which for the first time allowed the people to criticize their rulers? Where else but in English-speaking countries was there *habeas corpus*, which put an end to imprisonment without trial? Where else was there free speech, a free press and trial by jury? Further liberties would have followed in due course, without the spilling of blood."

And Joe, who loved and admired his father above all other men, accepted this. It did cross his mind, though, that for a peace-loving man, Papa had certainly done a splendid job on those two seamen! The rest of the way home he thought over the recent adventure, recalling with guilt how he had been ready to put his boot to the backside of a loyal Briton. Instantly he excused himself. Anyone who offered to hurt an old man who had done him no harm richly deserved a hiding!

Joe's blood was thoroughly British, but a warm heart insisted on fair play. For him, choosing between patriotism and justice was not always to be an easy task.

Born on December 13, 1804, Joe was the youngest child of John Howe and his second wife, widowed Mary Austen. By the time he was eight, most of his numerous half-brothers and half-sisters had married and left the low-roofed cottage on the Northwest Arm, two miles from Halifax. There were then only Joe and his parents, his older sister Sarah, and his grown-up half-sister Jane living at home. "Those were the days," he wrote wistfully in later life, "the wonderful days before love or work or ambition, and their memory will stay with me all my life, as vivid as sunlight."

He had all a boy could want – salt-water swimming and small boats at the front door, woods alive with wild creatures at the back. There was a brook where he could fish for trout and a mossy stone wall on which he could lie and dream. There was a stable where he and his friends could bury themselves in sweet-smelling hay and listen to the tales of an old soldier turned stableman. This man, and no one seems to recall his name or where he came from, taught Joe to box and wrestle and shoot, to ride a horse and sail a boat.

There was little yet to show what Joe would do or be. He was sturdy and quick, with blue eyes and a pale complexion which seldom tanned. His head, covered with wiry, light brown hair, was a trifle on the large side as was his nose. He was not a handsome boy, yet by most accounts there was something very attractive about him. He made friends easily and kept many of them all his stormy life. Among boys his own age he was generally the leader, good at sports and fonder of teasing the girls than of doing lessons. Yet he could study when he wished, and soon discovered an appetite for learning, an appetite fed by Father and Jane, who started him early on the Bible and Shakespeare. He possessed an excellent memory and could quote long passages of poetry by heart. This, from *Richard II*, was a favourite:

This royal throne of kings,
This sceptred Isle,
This earth of majesty, this seat of Mars ...
This blessed plot, this earth, this realm, this England.

He was well-drilled in grammar and mathematics, but history was his best subject. Papa and Jane answered his endless questions and encouraged his efforts to write verse. He knew there would be no money to send him to college. His only formal education would be perhaps a year at the local grammar school, and then, like his half-brother John, he would go to work at *Royal Gazette* and Post Office.

"One good thing," he told Jane with satisfaction, "I won't have to study any more."

She gave him a wise smile. "If you're sensible, Joe dear, you'll never stop studying all your life long." And, as a matter of fact, he never did. He soaked up knowledge wherever and whenever it could be found. "I know the value of education," he used to say, "from the lack of it." Jane Howe, a gentle dark-haired girl, daughter of John Howe's first wife, was at this time in her early twenties. None of her letters to Joe can be found and we know her mainly through his verse and letters he wrote to her. He spoke of her when he was in his sixties as "Jane, who next to my good wife and children, of all other beings on this earth I most dearly love." He wrote to her wherever he went and told her all that happened to him and how he felt about it.

His mother he mentions with respect in a verse which begins:

My mother, who my faults would chide,
With cares domestic on her brow ...

Though he may not have loved her as he loved Jane, he owed her a good deal, for she seems to have bequeathed to him that methodical common sense which so well balanced the idealism handed down to him by his father. In a home, moreover, where income was small and charity large, Mary Austen Howe's common sense was a valuable commodity.

These two women may have shaped Joe's view of womankind in general. Joe was never shy of the opposite sex and,

14

though fully aware of their charms, was able also to appreciate their mental and moral qualities.

In his eighth year, his pleasant world was thrown into a state of alarm when a British frigate, attacked at sea by an American squadron, limped into Halifax Harbour with wounded and dead members of the crew. When the formal declaration of war came next day, June 27, 1812, Joe's startled town prepared for invasion. The Halifax militia was called out and letters of marque – permission from the government to private ship owners to attack enemy ships – were issued to local merchant captains, who promptly turned their vessels into privateers. The House of Assembly voted £52,000 to repair the Citadel and arm the harbour batteries. The Navy brought shiploads of British soldiers to Halifax, who soon outnumbered the citizens on the town streets, but they were few enough when one remembered that British naval strength was stretched to its limit fighting Napoleon in Europe. Unless the Atlantic sea lanes could be kept open, the scattered northern colonies would almost certainly fall to the Americans. The effect of all this on Joe was tremendous. What horrified him most was the fact that the Americans were on the side of the French tyrant.

"But they're British!" he cried incredulously, "or their fathers were! How can they fight against Britain?"

"They're Americans now, lad," John Howe said with a sigh, "nursing old grudges, and possibly new ambitions." Though officially the Americans claimed that, as neutrals, their ships should not be stopped on the high seas, it was known they carried goods to supply Napoleon's armies and employed deserters from the British Navy. A Washington journalist stated it bluntly: "Let us liberate the British colonies and consolidate all North America under the Stars and Stripes."

Reading this, Joe felt his heart stir with fury. So those republicans planned to take over British North America, did they? They thought they could make an American out of Joe Howe, did they? Oh, if only he were old enough to fight! He pictured himself in the uniform of an admiral, a commodore at the very least, standing on the bridge of a British man-of-war, shouting: "Steady, my gallant tars! Ready! Fire!"

For two years the war ran haphazardly over half the continent, from Montreal to Maryland and from Nova Scotia to Niagara, with small profit to either side. The Americans invaded and were thrown back from Montreal, the British invaded and were thrown back from Detroit. The Americans burned York and the British burned Washington. The French, contrary to American hopes, stood by the British in Lower Canada; the Americans, expected to quail before the might of Britain's navy, surprisingly won most of the early sea and lake battles.

The course of the war changed in 1813 when H.M.S. *Shannon* captured U.S.S. *Chesapeake* in a single-ship duel off Boston. Joe and his cousin, Joe Letson, were hurried off to town that day in the Letson wagon to watch the arrival of the two gallant ships and never forgot the sight. The defeat of Napoleon in 1814 meant British aid could be sent more generously to her colonies, and a peace was arranged. Neither side had won, but Joe was sure Britain had, just as every red-blooded American boy was certain the war had been won by the States.

One thing, however, had been made clear. The northern colonists, including those of French blood, had shown even less desire than in 1776 to become Americans. The war had hardened feeling against the United States and had drawn closer together the small group of provinces which would one day form the nucleus of a new nation called Canada.

The peace treaty was signed just after Joe's tenth birthday. "The war's over," he rejoiced with Papa and Jane, "and we won. Imagine, if we'd lost, we've have turned into lawless rebels doing just as we pleased."

Jane laughed. "Joe dear, law and order exist in the States."

"They do?" He was astonished. "But they're a republic." He spoke the word with distaste. To the son of a Loyalist, it was a bad word—like democracy—an anti-British word related to violence and disorder rather than lawful self-government. "They govern *themselves*."

"A republic," Jane told him, "is merely a state in which the people, through elected representatives, have some say in how they are governed. England has had representative assemblies for hundreds of years – and ever since 1688, parliament (which is composed of the Sovereign, Lords and Commons) has governed Britain. Today however, the House of Commons has the most power, because it can raise taxes and vote, or not vote, money to the public departments of government. And it's the Commons who represents the people. So you see Britons govern themselves too."

Joe looked thoughtful. "Then I've been a republican all my life and didn't know it." Seeing their smiles, he protested. "I'm British and you say Britons govern themselves, just like the Americans."

"Not just like –" began Mr. Howe, then left it to his daughter to explain shades of difference in the meaning of the word. Jane did her best. "The United States, Joe, is a *republic*. England is a *monarchy*, with a representative form of government. They are both republican in the sense that they hold power by the votes of the people. Nova Scotia, however, is far from being a republic. We are a colony, you see, governed by the king through a colonial office and a lieutenant-governor."

"A colony isn't governed the same as Britain?" he asked, surprised.

"Well no, it isn't, Joe, because – well, because we're a colony."

How did crossing the ocean, he wondered, make a Briton any less a Briton?

"There are reasons for this, Joseph," his father said. "The American revolution, for instance, showed us that colonies could have too much legislative power. But for that, they might never have cast off their allegiance to Britain."

Joe still didn't understand. He knew vaguely how the British provinces were governed. Each had a lieutenant-governor sent out from Britain to represent His Majesty, a Council of local gentlemen appointed to help him, and a House of Assembly elected by the people, to represent *them*. "The governor is like the king," he said, "the Assembly is like the House of Commons, and the Council is like the House of Lords – so our government *must* be like the one at Home."

17

Jane gathered her wits to explain where the difference lay. "Actually, Joe, Nova Scotia has *two* Councils – the Executive Council, which takes care of Nova Scotia's daily affairs, and the Legislative Council which acts as the Upper House of the Legislature, the Assembly being the Lower. Together they make the laws. Mr. Jeffrey, the Customs Collector, for instance, and Sir Rupert George, our Provincial Secretary, not only run their departments – they sit in the Legislative Council and decide what bills sent up to them by the Assembly shall be passed and become law and which must be vetoed – that is, disallowed. Governor and Council represent the Crown, you see, and must be able to veto laws which might endanger the Crown's rights. But the Assembly has the right to raise taxes and refuse money to the government departments if the Council should be unfair or unreasonable, so you see it's all quite fair. One acts as a check on the other." Then, seeing the subject was a little beyond his present understanding, she gave him a hug and said reassuringly, "you'll understand better as you grow older."

He had one more question though. "Is it better to have a written constitution than an unwritten one?" He was jealous of something the Americans had that Britons lacked.

"The Americans think so," was Jane's answer, "but we feel it is better to be flexible, to let government evolve naturally as needed."

"Evolve?"

"Grow. Change by natural process, slowly and peacefully, rather than by devising a set of rigid rules, or by revolution which brings with it violence and misery. Think of it as a plant, Joe. The seed was the Greek idea that ordinary citizens – or some of them – should be allowed a voice in their city's government. Planted and watered and warmed by the sun, this seed brought forth in the time of Edward First of England, the bloom of representative government, a way for all the people to be represented, no matter if they lived near or far from the seat of government. Over the years, this plant grew additional leaves and buds and it will go on growing, bringing forth new and better blooms all the time when they are wanted."

"If some day, for example, Joseph, it is thought the colony can handle more responsibility, His Majesty will doubtless listen to our appeals and grant what we require," said his father. "Meanwhile we have all we need, a brave and generous governor, twelve wise and experienced councillors, a worthy and honest Assembly."

When John Howe had come to Halifax as a refugee long ago, Nova Scotia's government had been good to him. Finding him able and loyal, it had overlooked his peculiar religious views and made him Deputy Postmaster General as well as King's Printer. Magistrate Howe still ran the Post Office and published the government's *Royal Gazette*, with the help of his son John, yet even without these good things, loyal John Howe would have believed without question that the British province of Nova Scotia was ruled by the best of systems and the wisest of men.

But was this true?

It sounded fine in theory, but how did it work in practice?

CHAPTER TWO
1815-1820

"These ruffians of municipal authority ... "

Wilkie's Pamphlet, 1820

John Howe may have had his eyes closed to the faults of Nova Scotia's government but he was wide awake to the needs of his fellow man. Many came to his home for help and few left without it. Wherever he went he carried sweets in his pocket for the children and at one store in town the owner was under orders to supply packets of tea, sugar and flour at Mr. Howe's expense to certain needy families. One of his charitable customs was to visit the Bridewell Jail each Sabbath morning, to read scripture to the inmates, and Joe often accompanied him.

One Sunday shortly after the end of the war, Joe visited the Bridewell for the first time in several months and was struck by its mean appearance. What a decrepit and dirty place it was! A two-storey wooden structure, it had been built in the early days of the town as a barracks. Iron bars had been fastened to the windows, but they looked rusty and loose, and streaks of damp on the walls suggested a roof in need of repair. Even a ten year-old boy could see that the Bridewell was being neglected. Who was to blame? Not the jailors, Joe knew, because they could act only on orders from the Jail Commissioner. Halifax in that day had no mayor or aldermen, only magistrates appointed by governor and Council to supervise the town's courts and public works. The Jail Commissioner was one of these.

The door was unlocked by the head jailor, who gave them a surly greeting. He was never pleased to see the Howes. Other magistrates were content when they had tried a man and saw him hustled off to jail, but this interfering Sandemanian had to come poking his nose in every Sunday. He was even known to take released prisoners home with him, and feed and shelter them until they found work. Soft, that's what he was.

Accustomed by now to the odour of drains, stale food, and unwashed humanity, Joe followed his father into the large room where the prisoners sat huddled on benches against one wall. While Mr. Howe read from the Psalms, Joe studied the mixed lot of men, women, and children in tattered, dirty clothing. Some listened eagerly while others slumped against the wall, dull and listless. And no wonder, thought the boy, when they hardly ever saw the sun or breathed fresh air. Was it true, as gossip had it, that the jailors used these people like servants, beating them when they were disobedient? Surely a good and watchful supervisor would not let such things happen.

Their crimes did not seem so very serious to Joe. There were men here condemned to months of imprisonment for stealing a few potatoes from a rich man's garden. Child apprentices, guilty only of running away from a cruel master, received the same treatment as adults confined for fighting in the streets or stealing. Naturally prison couldn't be a house of pleasure. It was intended to reform those who broke the law. But, looking around him that day, Joe thought it might have quite the opposite effect.

He slipped out during the prayer and, by comparison, the yard with its barn and chicken-house odours, smelled sweet and clean. He went looking for a friend, Matt the Lamplighter, a spirited old fellow, jailed regularly for drunkenness, but Joe liked him because he always stood up to adversity with a joke and a grin. Matt hadn't appeared for the scripture reading and Joe wondered if he'd been released. No, there he was at the woodpile, splitting logs with frowning concentration. Around his bare old throat, digging into the flesh, was the spiked dog-collar used as punishment for minor offences around the jail. Joe rushed over, crying angrily – "What's that for?"

The old man straightened, wiped an arm across his sweat-grimed face. There was no humour in him today. He gave the boy an unsmiling glance, then bent to toss the split log aside.

"Nothing to be done," he muttered.

"What did you do?" Everyone knew there was no harm in old Matt. Even the underkeepers indulged him for the sake of his cheerful jokes. Angrily, Joe answered his own question: "Nothing! Someone's being a bully!"

"Hush, boy" Matt said anxiously, and at that moment the head jailor came out of the barn's shadow.

"Work, you old fool, or you'll get worse," he shouted as he passed. He gave Joe a look too, as if to say "And the same to you if you weren't the magistrate's boy."

The old man set a new log in place, muttering over his shoulder: "Go 'way, Joe, nothing to be done," and chopped as if his life depended on it.

The minute the door closed behind them, Joe poured out his tale and saw his father's face cloud. "I don't understand it," he confessed. "I have complained about that jailor several times. A few weeks ago, he kept a woman in the stocks all night because she pushed him away when he was too familiar. When the Commissioner could not see his way clear to discharging the man, I put the case before the Sessions, but they said nothing could be done."

Hearing the echo of Matt's words, Joe stared at his father in consternation. The Jail Commissioner had the right and the duty, surely, to discharge brutal jailors.

"They tell me I am too easy," John Howe said, "and perhaps that is so. Someone, I know, must deal firmly with convicted criminals, but as I grow older I fear I lean more to mercy than justice."

"Justice! Where is the justice in letting an old man be ill-treated? I'd like to knock that jailor's brains out!"

"Foolish talk, Joseph." His father's voice grew stern. "Authority must be respected. Order must be kept. Otherwise, we would live like beasts in the jungle. I shall of course report this to the Sessions." By the Sessions, John Howe meant the quar-

John Howe Junior (1784-1843) half-brother of Joe Howe.

terly gathering of magistrates to hear and judge complaints on matters which concerned the town. "Something will be done."

"And if something *isn't* done?"

"We do our best," the magistrate said quietly, and this silenced Joe. It was true Papa did his best, serving as magistrate without pay or gift, simply out of a sense of duty, but what about the other magistrates? And how would taking strong action against a jailor lead to Halifax becoming a jungle?

There was something strange here. Perhaps another of those grown-up secrets a boy was always coming up against. Well, he would not be a child much longer, and when he was a man he'd know everything and would see that the magistrates did their duty.

Five years later, a young man named Will Wilkie got into serious trouble trying to do that very thing.

Joe was fifteen the year Wilkie wrote and published his abusive pamphlet accusing the town magistrates of putting people in jail for trivial offences in order to collect the fees, and of accepting money from well-to-do prisoners to release them. For his pains, young Wilkie was brought by the magistrates to trial to answer to a charge of libel – the crime of publishing material damaging to the reputation of public men.

Joe had, by this time, been at work two years in the *Royal Gazette* printing shop under his half-brother, John Howe Jr., a married man in his late thirties. On his father's retirement, John had succeeded to the offices of King's Printer and Postmaster. This was the way things were done in that day. Jobs stayed in families, descending from father to son and then to grandson, as long as they did nothing to displease governor or Council. Joe knew he could, if he wished, look forward to one of these posts when he was older. At the moment, having graduated from devil – the boy who ran errands, swept floors, and cleaned out the candlesticks each morning – he was learning the mysteries of type and press. Although he worked an average of twelve hours a day, he was not allowed time off to attend the trial. For one reason, it was a case which had aroused a great demand for gallery seats. Libel cases were rare in the British provinces. The younger John Howe, himself a magistrate, was there of course. He was there also to report the story for the newspaper.

John was not surprised, when he returned late that afternoon, to find his young brother waiting with impatience to hear the verdict. "Did he get off?"

"I should say not! The young idiot refused a lawyer and made a wild speech in his own defence which was even more inflammatory than the pamphlet. He gave judge and jury no choice."

"He's young." Joe reached for a cloth to clean his ink-stained hands. "There's no harm in him."

"I disagree, Joe. Such people can be dangerous." John, like his father, seldom saw faults in government. "The fellow was given every chance to apologize." But an apology, thought Joe shrewdly, would sound as though Wilkie were withdrawing his charges. Poor Wilkie. It was a first offence, though. He'd probably get off with a fine.

The sentence, handed down a few days later, shocked both brothers.

"Two years!" Joe was appalled.

"A stern sentence," John agreed solemnly, "but necessary. The peace of the community must not be broken by criticism of authority. To overlook such attacks could lead to anarchy, as it did in the case of the Thirteen Colonies. I pity Wilkie's parents. They're very decent, respectable folk."

But all Joe's pity was reserved for the brave, foolish young man doomed to spend two years of his life in that filthy Bridewell. Several of the charges in the pamphlet, Joe suspected, were mild compared with what actually went on in the jail. He could now make a fair guess at why, five years ago, the head jailor had not worried about being called to account for his brutalities. He and the Jail Commissioner protected each other, and the Sessions seldom judged a fellow magistrate harshly. As to the severity of the sentence, there might be a reason for that too. Judge Blowers was a member of His Majesty's Council, and Wilkie had accused the Council of refusing to pass a bill because it conflicted with the interests of that body.

The crack of doubt which had opened for Joe as a small boy, now opened wider. It was not so wide as to make a Reformer out of him, but wide enough to leave a lasting impression.

However, for the next four years, Joe had little time to think of Wilkie or the Bridewell. He was too busy preparing himself for a suitable career.

CHAPTER THREE
1820-1828

"This is my year of suspense."

Letter to Jane
November 18, 1824

By 1824 Joe, a confident, energetic young man of twenty, was a well-known figure around Halifax town. He wore the new-fashioned tight "trowsers" and a collar so high it scraped his chin, smoked a long white clay pipe, carried a short cane, and knew all the latest ribald stories. His eyes, full of life and curiosity, looked directly from under a pair of eyebrows which, twisting upwards at their outer corners, gave him a look of deviltry and arrogance, softened by a mouth generous and full of humour.

He had friends in all walks of life, and was much in demand at dinners and dancing parties, also at games. He and his brother William Howe were Garrison champions at racquets, a fast bat-and-ball game much like tennis, played against a wall rather than over a net, a game coming into great popularity at that time. A purely social life, however, was not for Joe.

"This is my year of suspense," he wrote Jane in an idle hour at the Post Office. His half-sister Jane was now Mrs. William Austen and lived in New Brunswick, but the tie between them remained strong. He confessed to her that he was dissatisfied, consumed by a restless, agitating uncertainty. "I am something like a poor devil of a traveller who finds himself at the entrance of three or four roads, not knowing which to take." He was not just marking time though; he was preparing himself as well as he could for what might crop up some day in the way of opportunity. He had begun a heavy study course, mostly on his own. He read history by the light of the kitchen fire until the small hours and regularly practised speaking French with a relative, because he believed that any man or woman who cared about culture ought to speak both languages. He was an avid reader of the classics, of poetry and plays. He attended lectures and concerts whenever he could. With all this, he took care to keep in good shape physically with regular riding, boxing, fishing and hunting. "If only I could be content," he wrote Jane wistfully, "to go along quietly and peaceably like my neighbours and at the end of some fifty or sixty years tumble into my grave and be dust, I should be happy, very happy." Knowing her brother, Jane smiled at this passage. She couldn't imagine anything less pleasing to Joe than a life like that. "But this infernal feeling," he went on, "whatever it be, still points to something ahead which is viewless and undefined."

Was he to be a stifled, ill-paid public servant all his life like John and Father, or could he find the courage to cut loose, strike out on a new path altogether? In the United States, so he had heard, men as educationally limited as himself were making fortunes. His friend, Tom Haliburton, however, insisted he forget a business career. "Stick to the arts. That's where your talents lie." True, Joe's verses were now appearing in print with some regularity, and Tom ought to know – he too was writing verse and also humour, while practising his profession as a lawyer.

Looking back five years to the Wilkie trial, Joe saw that what had happened in the next ten months had marked the end of his boyhood. Jane had married and moved to Saint John. Sarah had gone to visit her and had there met the man she promptly married. They had then set out immediately for England, and Joe had been bereft. He and Sarah had grown closer after Jane's marriage, and he missed her almost as much as Jane. Perhaps partly for this reason, he embarked on a period of reckless self-indulgence, putting aside self-improvement and behaving in ways typical of youth. It was probably during this time that he fathered his illegitimate son, Edward. His enemies would mention the existence of this child to show what an immoral and irresponsible fellow Joe Howe was, yet surely the opposite was true. He took his paternal responsibility seriously and eventually the mother, whoever she was and for whatever reason, left the boy entirely in his care. Edward Howe became what he remained until his death in middle age, an accepted and valued member of Joe's own family.

Edward's birth may have sobered Joe, because by 1823 he had turned his abundant energies from poetry and mischief to the serious business of earning a living. So well did he handle this, he soon became his brother's trusted second-in-command and was often left in complete charge of both *Gazette* and Post Office.

This was a time of serious financial depression, and Joe could see the suffering caused by war and unemployment. Poor folk had it hard and, without the town's several charitable societies, many no doubt would have died. Judges, bishops, and councillors contributed to these charities, but they could still enjoy their country estates, their carriages and balls; and a few men, like Enos Collins, prospered in spite of everything. Having made his first fortune as a wartime privateersman, Collins was now working on his second as the local banker and had become a prominent member of Council.

Joe enjoyed his work on the whole, but Post Office and *Royal Gazette* together took up only half his time and energy, and he was often bored and restless. As he told Jane, "Being the servants of government, we cannot extend our concern in any way so as to make more employment and more profit."

The sudden clatter of a cantering horse and its snorting arrival in front of the open window of the Post Office cut into his thoughts. He saw that the rider was no less a personage than the colony's latest Governor, Sir James Kempt, and that His Excellency was in a fine rage. Leaning over his horse's head, the Governor shouted for the Postmaster. Joe explained with respect that his brother was out, and offered his own assistance. Peevishly, Sir James began a complaint about his letters and when John Howe, Senior, came to see if he too could help, the Governor turned on the old gentleman and berated him as if the fault had been his. Joe's temper came very near the surface. "I felt," he wrote years later, "like knocking him off his horse." Angry words trembled on his lips, but the look on his father's face stopped him. Mr. Howe seemed quite unaware of any rudeness, retaining his usual air of dignity and composure, which had its effect on Sir James too. His voice softened. "Tell your son, sir, to be more careful in future."

When he had ridden off, Joe said with disgust: "And I thought all governors were gentlemen." He had never before looked at his sovereign's representative with anything but awed reverence. Father, however, would hear no ill spoken of Sir James, saying His Excellency no doubt felt the wound in his leg; a wound, he reminded his son, suffered at Waterloo.

"We cannot enjoy here the free expression of our sentiments," Joe wrote with exasperation, "and are not infrequently subject to the caprice of men in office." He said he had never liked this sort of thing as a boy, and as a man was determined that he would not put up with it.

The solution of course was to strike out on his own.

But in which direction? John suggested he study law. "You could indenture with a local firm, like your friend Lawrence Doyle, and five years from now pass the Bar, with nothing more to worry about." Though the law held small charm for him, Joe knew the advice was good. Lawyers usually went into the Assembly or Council and then became judges, making a good deal of money in the process. Joe agreed to think about it, but in the back of his mind was a dream of owning a newspaper, one in which he would be free to express his own views. He did invest a small sum the following year in a paper published at Miramichi, New Brunswick. The fact that the venture lasted only a year may have been due, in part at least, to the terrible Miramichi Fire of that year.

Recently, another possibility had presented itself. He had received a letter from Sarah saying she and her husband were planning to move to South America where business prospects looked brighter. Why didn't Joe consider going there too? He was tempted. He would, of course, have to borrow for the journey, and he hated going into debt in such uncertain times.

There was another very good reason for him to settle soon on a career. Her name was Susan Ann. She lived on a large, heavily-wooded island at the mouth of Halifax Harbour. It is still called McNabs' and looks much the same today as it did in 1827. It was owned by a member of Council, a gentleman-farmer named Peter McNab the Second. Susan Ann was his niece. She and her brother James, both born in Newfoundland where their father Captain John McNab had been stationed during the war, had come with their parents to live on the family island when Susan Ann was ten. The hospitable stone house of the McNabs in the past had entertained important visitors like the Duke of Kent and his brother Prince William; now it welcomed humbler friends like John Howe and his family. Where and when Joe first met Susan Ann or when he became seriously interested in her, we do not know. "Thou wert the guiding star," he wrote later in life, "whose living beam flash'd o'er Youth's troubled thoughts." At any rate, by 1827 he was making regular visits to McNabs' Island.

"Glide merrily on, my little skiff," he sang as he rowed, "o'er waves lit up by Luna's smile," and, since it was a good two-mile row, he had time to compose a further couplet –

> If Fate bestow, I'll ask no more
> Than her who lives on yonder Isle.

Fate did not, however, quickly bestow Susan Ann McNab on Joseph Howe. The McNabs would hardly encourage the match, much as they may have liked the bright-eyed youth with the unruly eyebrows. They may even have seen qualities in him not yet apparent to others, but they were members of an old and influential family and Susan Ann was their only daughter. She was pretty and affectionate, sang nicely and excelled at fine needlework. She was also intelligent. She could have her pick of army and navy officers or the sons of wealthy councillors. Why set her heart on a low-salaried civil servant like Joe Howe, bright enough in his way, but never likely to rise higher than the minor government posts now occupied by his half-brothers. They must have talked to their daughter in this kindly way, hoping to make her see reason, while Joe with a jealous eye on the army and navy officers looked anxiously about for a way to make money and become an acceptable suitor to the McNabs.

He gave the South American idea more serious consideration. When a second letter arrived from Sarah saying they were about to sail for Peru, he wrote that the moment he had word of their arrival in South America, he would set out from Halifax. He would make his fortune as quickly as he could, then hurry back and lay it at Susan Ann's feet.

Tragically, when word finally came from Peru, it was to announce Sarah's death on the voyage.

It was the first hard blow of Joe's life, a blow which fell even harder on his parents. They were old. He, the last of their large family, could not now with an easy conscience think of leaving them. They would feel sure that if he too went off, they would never see him again. So all thought of leaving Nova Scotia was given up, and Joe made a deliberate effort to attach himself to his own little backward British province. "As the probability of my ever seeing any other has vanished," he wrote Jane, "it is daily becoming more dear to me."

Perhaps the tragedy softened the McNabs, or possibly quiet persistence on Susan Ann's part had its effect, for the two families put their heads together and came up with a plan. William Minns, brother of Mr. Howe's first wife, a friend or connection of the McNabs as well, was growing too old to run his weekly newspaper. It was suggested that Joe take it over in partnership with James Spike, a cousin of the Howes who also worked at the *Gazette*. This would provide a respectable and safe future for their daughter. It was not quite what Joe wanted, but with Susan Ann as the prize, he did not hesitate. He agreed, with Spike, to buy the paper on easy terms.

The first issue of the *Acadian* may be read today in the files of the Nova Scotia Archives. It consists of four pages, much of it written by its youthful editor. The opening editorial was Joe's first public utterance of his aims and his paper's devotion to Nova Scotia and loyalty to the Crown. "Born and reared upon the soil of Nova Scotia, our earliest and fondest associations are naturally twined round our native land ... Warmly attached to the Mother Country by a firm conviction of the blessings we enjoy as an important portion of her Dominions, we shall ever lend our best exertions to strengthen and perpetuate the connection."

A letter to sister Jane around this time sounds happy and confident: "Under the editorial shelter of that great battery 'we,' I thunder away as much nonsense as my contemporaries, write long leading articles upon subjects about which I know nothing, and speculate most gravely upon political changes and affairs of state."

Over the next eight months his writing rapidly improved, showing a strength and vitality lacking in his verse. With young John away in England that year, Joe had nearly the whole of the work and responsibility of the Post Office, *Royal Gazette*, and Father's literary *Journal*, as well as the *Acadian*, though Spike took most of the printing off his hands and Father helped with the editorials. He still found time though to visit McNab's island, to walk on the curving beach with his hazel-eyed lass and recite poetry to her.

"Although I have given up the idea of ever being rich," he wrote Jane, "yet I do not despair that the same industry and activity of mind which, if exerted in a wider field, might have made me so, will at least earn for me a moderate independence." And he bragged that, in addition to retaining all but four of Mr. Minn's subscribers, he had got one hundred and twenty more.

Yet he was not content.

Working in double harness did not suit him. The minds of others seldom kept pace with his, and there were times when Spike's slowness and caution irritated him almost past bearing. Then one day, in the autumn of 1828, a piece of news electrified him. George Young, editor and owner of the *Novascotian*, had decided to study for the law and was offering his paper for sale. The *Novascotian* was bigger and brighter than the *Acadian* and had more than twice the circulation. George would want at least a thousand pounds for it. If he bought it – and this was the daring thought in Joe's head – he would be taking a heavy gamble.

He had no savings. He would have to give up his jobs at the *Gazette* and Post Office and sell his share of the *Acadian* for what little it was worth. He had had barely a year's experience in independent news publishing, and he wanted to marry. The McNabs had agreed with reluctance to a son-in-law with a small but safe income. They might think this new venture far too risky for their daughter to share.

He would have to borrow. The paper might fail. The one in New Brunswick had failed.

No! The *Novascotian*, under his care, would flourish and grow like the green bay tree! It would be a howling success!

When he found Susan Ann shared his confidence, the thing was settled. He went to see Young and afterwards talked it over with his father, who sat down and wrote to his friend, Captain McNab: "As I know you and Mrs. McNab are deeply interested in my son Joseph's prosperity and welfare and may be anxious as to the propriety of the step which he will inform you he has taken, I conceive it my duty to acquaint you that in all he has my perfect concurrence." The McNabs agreed to the marriage.

"On Saturday morning," we read in several of the Halifax papers under *Marriages*, "by the Venerable Archdeacon Willis, Mr. Joseph Howe to Miss Catherine Susan Ann McNab, only daughter of Captain McNab." Though neither bride nor groom were members of the Anglican church, they had to be married by the rector of St. Paul's, for the Anglican church was at that time the only denomination in Nova Scotia licensed to perform marriages. Here was an example of the unfairness of the colonial system, but at that time Joe was too happy to worry about it.

The marriage of Joe and Susan Ann appears to have been a resounding success, an active partnership and a love match in which Susan Ann, carried into stormier waters than she may have expected, never disappointed her husband nor faltered in her love. As for him, the hundreds of letters he wrote her in the course of his much-travelled life bear witness to the closeness between them. She helped in the print shop and dealt with creditors when he was away, often when there was not a dollar in the house to pay them. She entertained his political friends, kept his home, and gave him ten children.

The young couple settled down after the ceremony in a small house near the shop – only the very wealthy in those days could afford a wedding trip – and soon after, Joe's small son Edward came to live with them.

The one year of suspense had stretched to nearly five, but at last Joe's life had begun in earnest, or, as he put it to Jane in a letter written just after the marriage – "I began the world only a year and a half ago, at which time my goods and chattels were not perhaps worth more than five pounds. Having trust in Providence and, as you know I always had, a modest reliance on my own head and hands, I have now saddled myself with a wife and an obligation to pay £1,050 within five years." And this was in a period of financial depression in a province where cash was short at the best of times.

But the suspenseful years had not been wasted in idleness and vain imaginings. He was starting out with good equipment – tried experience and a willingness to work, not just debts and hope.

It may be that he told his bride, as they set their small home in order what he would tell her a thousand times in the years of their life together –

"All will be well. Have no fears."

But by the spring of 1828, despite hard work and frugal living, the young Howes had to face the fact that without heroic measures, the paper would go under.

CHAPTER FOUR
1828

"For many years the newspaper press must be the great medium of instruction to the people."

Novascotian, January, 1828

Cash was urgently needed, and Joe knew only one way to get it. He must comb the province for monies owed the paper. He could at the same time try to sell advertising and canvass for new subscriptions. Reluctant to leave the paper for several months in the sole care of two inexperienced boys, he was pleased when his wife offered diffidently to help. He had a high opinion of Susan Ann's tact and talent and was, besides, surprisingly modern in his view that women ought not to be confined to bedroom and kitchen but should be companions to their husbands, with intellects and wider interests than just the home. He therefore delegated to her the supervision of small Edward, the direction of the apprentices, the reading of proofs and the paying of bills when there was money to do so. Then, with a light heart, he embarked on what he described in the *Novascotian* as his *Western Ramble*.

His first tour through the western counties covered most of the Annapolis Valley as far as Church Point, a village on the French Shore. Sometimes he was lucky and travelled by one of the new stagecoaches, in which case he always rode on the roof so he would have the best view. "Crack goes the whip," he wrote in his first *Ramble* article, "and away you roll on your journey, wondering at the rapidity of your motion and the motion of the coach." He had cause to marvel, for the roads were mostly ruts and mud puddles. The coach, supported by leather straps, not steel springs, had a tendency to roll sideways as well as forward and back, and so, at the high average speed of six miles an hour, the passengers were tossed about in all directions. Joe rode each toss and roll with the ease of the practised horseman, banging on the roof in his exuberance, startling the inside-passengers and urging them to admire the scenery.

Where the coaches did not go, along side paths and through the forest, Joe hired a horse or, where it was too rough for a horse, he walked. And, as he covered the miles in his cheerful, inquisitive way, he was happy and knew it, which is rare among humans, and grateful for his happiness, which is rarer still.

One day passing through sunlit woods he was filled with a kind of awe and tenderness for the world around him. How beautiful it all was! Small brooks ran up out of the underbrush and chuckled along beside him for a mile or two. The gleam of a placid lake enticed him to a quick swim. Small creatures rustled in the grass. Birds sang. "I didn't pray," he wrote Susan Ann that night, "but my heart was full to overflowing for the goodness and mercy of Him who created me and has sustained me thus far on life's journey." The calm forest, he said, had done more to strengthen the better feelings and nobler impulses of his nature than forty parsons could have done with forty sermons. "I cannot think when I had such a day's enjoyment. Now do not turn up your little nose and pucker up your lips at this confession, for the delight and solace springing from the society of my own Susan Ann are to be thought of and regarded apart from all other earthly gratifications."

He told her the paper looked very well. A few spelling mistakes, perhaps, but that was a small matter. "You are doing fine, my little editress. I wish I could send more money, but cash is scarce, even amongst farmers well off in land and stock."

He wondered why this should be.

From what he had so far observed, Nova Scotia had every good thing needed for health, happiness and prosperity – good soil, in the valley at any rate, plenty of useful minerals, fish, lumber, and a short but excellent growing season. Yet much of the land lay fallow. Ditching and fencing were neglected. Farms, he had heard, were generally mortgaged. There was no cash changing hands and few settlements of any size. Hardly one contained a church or a mill or a post office. Too many men, he decided, sat idle when they should have been ploughing. Too many wives gossiped when they ought to have been gathering eggs or making butter.

The Nova Scotians were not working hard enough! They were not practising good husbandry! Someone should tell them so. This was a job for his paper. Henceforth the *Novascotian* would gently lecture his readers on their ways, then provide them with the latest information on agricultural methods. He would suggest that successful farmers write in and share with readers what they themselves had learned, and in this way, every farmhouse in the province could, with the *Novascotian* acting as supervisor, become a school. In a thousand different ways, in fact, he and his paper could work to raise the intellectual standards of the province. "My country may be small," he thought, "but some day, if I have anything to do with it, the very word 'Nova Scotian' will be a word of distinction! Britons will see that the good seed they sowed has fallen on fine soil, and the Americans will recognize in this little peninsula the home of a race superior to many, and second to none!" Discovering tears in his eyes, he was unashamed. His emotion was genuine. Still, being also a practical man, he repeated the last few sentences aloud, polished them a trifle, and committed them to memory for future use.

Though a stranger to the valley, Joe found a welcome wherever he went. At first, no doubt, the country folk were simply pleased to see a new face and to hear all the latest news of town, but they soon sensed his interest in them and responded by giving him their confidence. He had such easy, friendly ways, accepting the humblest hospitality with simple pleasure, eating heartily whatever was put before him, quick to lend a hand in barn or boat. He had no airs, would chase the littlest girl around the supper table until he caught and kissed her, and could keep everyone laughing for hours over his jokes and stories. But when the fun was over, when talk with the men around the fire grew serious and he tried to suggest, tactfully, how they might improve their livelihood, the grumblings began.

"Rich are we? I wish we were, but no matter how hard we work, we stay poor. Our best land lies idle. Why? Because large tracts are owned by Bishop Inglis and Brenton Halliburton and other Halifax men close to the governor and their fellow Loyalists on the Council. They don't trouble to cultivate the land because they're holding it for sale some day at a good profit."

"Then there's taxes," someone groaned.

"Taxes," Joe said firmly, "are lower here than anywhere else in British North America."

"Maybe so, but where does the money go? I'll tell you where it goes. It goes to Halifax to pay for public buildings like Government House and the new Citadel, or to Windsor to keep up Kings College for the sons of a few rich Anglicans –"

"Whilst our children," another burst in, "don't even have schools!"

Joe admitted this was bad. Though never a practising Sandemanian, he had absorbed many of the sect's beliefs, and one was that public money should not be spent on schools of one faith. "Teach your children, yourselves," he advised them. "Take any book that is handy and from it teach spelling and grammar at least. I do that with my apprentices after working hours, and you'd be surprised how quickly they learn. I've got one lad, an Irish boy named Whelan, who came here a penniless orphan only two years ago. He's now learning French and Latin. And remember, while teaching your children," – he looked around confidently – "keep working on your assemblyman to raise the issue of schools the next time he goes to Halifax."

They shook their heads. Unless you were a Loyalist and an Anglican, you didn't get schools or contracts or land or jobs. Dissenters had to get on as best they could, on their own. "Them in the Assembly," grunted a Bridgetown man, "do naught but talk. Oh, they bootlick us long enough to get elected, then forget us. Too busy sideling up to the bigwigs on the Council for favours! The Council's the only bunch can do anything for anybody, but they won't, not for us country folk, not for us Baptists and Catholics and Presbyterians.''

"The Assembly can do anything,'' Joe insisted, "if it has the sympathy and support of the people behind it.'' Here was another job for the *Novascotian*, to explain the government to the people and tell them what was being done by the House during its regular Sessions. That was the duty of the press, to pour out the information fairly and honestly. Then that knowledge could flow back at election time. "If you stand firmly behind your Member, show him what you want, and vote for him, the Assembly will have all the power it needs to offset the Council's.''

Certainly that was how government in the colony was supposed to work. What Joe did not yet see was that the Council, holding office for life by appointment and not by election, had grown in power through the years. Quietly, without undue fuss or noise, a small privileged group had managed to get all the good things – land, appointments, patronage – into their own hands until now they were firmly in control. To make things worse, the average Assemblyman, awed by the Council, deferred to it, sometimes in return for favours and sometimes at the people's expense. And this is how it was in all the British provinces, not just in Nova Scotia.

Joe, a young man of more than average perception, still did not see this. Loyal son of a loyal British father, he thought governors and members of Council appointed by His Majesty would never deliberately wrong the people. They might make a few honest mistakes, but these could be cured by a little energetic effort on the part of the people and their representatives.

And that is why Joe Howe went happily over the countryside preaching hard work and study as a cure-all for the country's ills.

His road lay next along the South Shore, though it could hardly be called a road. It was a path little better than an Indian trail with deep bogs on either side. A horse or man could plunge into them, he thought, and never be heard of again!

Along the way he caught up with an American peddler carrying on his shoulder a sack of small wares – needles and pins and ribbons and such – designed for the country-wife trade. The man was lame, having fallen through a rotten bridge the day before, so Joe gave him his horse to ride and walked alongside for a mile or two.

"Your country's awful backward," the peddler grumbled. "Everybody's half asleep. In the States we'd never put up with tracks like this or bridges like the one I went through yestiddy. Our free, republican citizens are ahead of you Britishers in every way, o'course – comes of being a democracy."

"It comes of having a long head start," Joe said tartly. "We'll catch up. As for democracy, we want none of that here."

The peddler shrugged, asking himself what good it was to try to help such backward-thinking people. Joe recovered his temper while giving the man a long lecture on the wealth and charm of Nova Scotia and the glory of belonging to the great British Empire. He may not have convinced the Yankee, but his eloquence left the man open-mouthed by the time they parted company.

Fault-finding, thought Joe, is not the answer. Complaint could lead, as in the States, to open rebellion. It was better to bear the few evils they knew than fly to others unknown. He had no use for grumblers or lukewarm patriots, lumping them all together under the word "radicals."

At Yarmouth next day, he met one of the breed. At first report, Herbert Huntington seemed just the sort of man Joe could admire. He was a successful farmer and fisherman who also found time to work for the community's school and library. Where could he find this admirable character, Joe wanted to know, and was directed to the Huntington fish-stage where he found the great man himself seated on a herring barrel with a short pipe between his teeth, figuring the day's catch on a shingle. Joe introduced himself and Huntington, a man of few words, pointed with his pipe to a second fish-barrel. After a brief exchange on crops and the weather, Joe began to speak with enthusiasm of the plans he had for curing Nova

Scotia's idleness and extravagance. Hungtington frowned.

"There'll be no improvements," he said, "until we improve our government."

"Sir Peregrine Maitland is not perhaps the strongest governor –" Joe began tolerantly, but was interrupted by a spate of words which shot from Huntington's mouth with the force of bullets.

"The governor doesn't matter. The Council runs the country and will go on doing so until we change the system."

Good lord, thought Joe, the man's a Radical!

"If the system's so bad," he retorted, "what would you put in its place?"

"The British constitution," the other answered at once, "in the same form they have it at home. We'll have no real political freedom in Nova Scotia until we have two distinct political parties in the House fighting out each issue in public debate, the one with the majority taking over all the offices of government."

Cabinet government? In a *colony*?

"It would amount to self-government," Joe exclaimed.

"So?"

"A colony can't rule itself."

"Why not? A group of twelve arrogant, self-interested irresponsible men run it now."

"Even if that were true, we've got an Assembly to check them."

"How? The Assembly meets once a year for a week or two. The Provincial Secretary and his fellow officials see each other every day of the year. They decide over tea in the governor's drawing-room what bills will be approved, get them passed with the help of their supporters in the House and confirm them behind closed doors in the Legislative Chamber. They then send the laws off to England to be approved by a friendly clerk in the colonial office. The House, when it meets again, finds that all its work has been done for them."

"It's not helpless though, Huntington. The House has the power of the purse. It can threaten the Council with loss of the annual revenue."

41

"Little good that does, when the executive officers can draw their own high salaries from mine royalties and customs duties, monies which ought never to have been designated Casual Revenues. When I am elected, Howe, and I mean to be at the next election, I shall work to have those Casual Revenues put under the control of the Assembly where they properly belong. Then the House will have some power. I shall also work for a more responsible system of government, one in which officers cannot hold their places for life."

"And I," said Joe with equal decision, "will continue to support the present constitution. Nothing must be allowed to endanger our connection with the Mother Country."

"I wish I were sure the Mother Country valued it as we do," Huntington said. Joe was shocked.

"She does, of course!"

Huntington's abstracted gaze fell on the barreled fish. "Sometimes," he said sombrely, "I think our only importance to her is as a source of cheap fish and lumber and a market for her manufactured goods."

"Ridiculous!"

"Is it? London industrialists don't have any sentimental notions about England's overseas children. They're businessmen first and last, caring only about profits. If and when they decide they can buy wood and fish cheaper from the States and sell to them at higher prices than they can to us, they'll make sure the British government lifts its high duties on American goods. Then we'll be forced to compete on an equal basis with a country far bigger and richer."

"Good," Joe said briskly. "We'll have free trade then. I've never believed in protectionism. I hate the artificial support of trade. Every pot should stand on its own bottom. We'll manage, with or without British duties on American products. We can make our own trade agreements – a reciprocity treaty, say, with the Americans."

"And then, as I told you, Britain may not care too much if the connection between us is broken."

Joe stared at the other man with disbelieving eyes. "What about our ports, man, and our fortifications? Britain needs us as much as we need her, especially if there's another war with the States."

"Forts and garrisons cost money. British merchants may baulk eventually at paying taxes to support them. I hope I'm as loyal a Briton as yourself, Howe, but I must believe that some day we'll be forced to go the way of the Americans."

"Not I then!" Joe cried fiercely.

"Perhaps not complete independence," the other amended, "but something close to it."

"I'll never believe it," Joe repeated with conviction. And so it went all afternoon, the two arguing and seldom agreeing. Yet this conversation began a friendship which lasted, in spite of differences, until Huntington's death twenty years later.

Joe rode home from Yarmouth a week later feeling pleased with his tour of the west. He had collected sufficient cash to see them through for the present. He had also got a great many new subscribers and made scores of new friends. No longer were the people of these counties simply names on a subscription list. No longer was he the unknown Mr. Editor. He and the Germans of Lunenburg had exchanged broad jokes over pork and sauerkraut. He and the canny New England farmers of the Valley had talked over new apple varieties and the best way to grow corn. With the Acadians of St. Mary's Bay and the Pubnico's he had tried out his stumbling French and they had understood each other very well. There were still the Scots and Irish of the north shore and the Yorkshire people of Cumberland, but these could wait until he had time to include them with Prince Edward Island and New Brunswick.

As he rode briskly homeward he thought of Huntington. A decent man, and intelligent, but a dangerous innovator, Joe thought, who might drag Nova Scotia into all sorts of mischief. Ever distrustful of untried theories, he visualized party government as suggested by Huntington, and saw in imagination the members of each party fighting like dogs for power without regard for the good of the country. Nova Scotia had more than enough violence as it was, particularly at election time! No, parties were out of the question. If there was one thing Joe prided himself on, it was his independence. "The *Novascotian* must never be found supporting a class, privileged *or* popular," he said proudly. "My party is Nova Scotia!"

Picture then his outrage when, on arriving home, he found a Montreal newspaper on his desk and read in it a letter from the *Colonial Patriot* of Pictou, describing him, Joe Howe, as a young man, formerly employed by the Post Office, therefore tied to a party and obliged to be servile to the Council. "The principles of the *Novascotian*," the letter said, "are notorious for the total absence of independence and all pretensions to it."

Wrathfully, Joe reached for quill and inkpot. "We defy the *Patriot* to quote one servile sentiment from our editorial columns," he wrote. "Evidently to a radical paper, a servile is anyone who will not hang the Council or roast the Assembly and will never stop thinking, talking and writing about the permanent grant for Pictou Academy." This was a dig at the man generally suspected of being the moving spirit behind the *Patriot*, a Scot named Thomas McCulloch, founder and principal of the Presbyterian Pictou Academy. Dr. McCulloch had been trying for years to secure a permanent grant for his Academy, without success, and this accounted, in Joe's opinion, for his hatred of the Council.

In its next issue, the *Patriot* replied that it had fully expected to be charged with radicalism. That had been the refuge of all supporters of abuses since the world began. "The Pharaoh no doubt considered Moses a great radical. The sturdy barons who forced the *Magna Carta* on King John were villainous radicals too, obviously." The editor invited the *Novascotian*'s editor to look at Upper and Lower Canada where there were well-organized parties both in and out of the legislature, whereas in Nova Scotia there was none, or only the well-organized party of the Twelve Councillors, who had easy times of it. "The day will come when there will be party against party."

"With party," the *Novascotian* shot back, "will come party spirit, which will soon prevail over duty and patriotism!"

"The best way to show patriotism," returned the *Patriot*, "is by advancing the interests of the King's subjects," and asked if it was fair that the Council, who were only twelve, should govern against the united desires of the whole population. "The root of the evil is the system, which makes it possible for all good things to be kept among the Council members and their families."

The two papers then descended to name-calling.

"Envious partisans," sniffed the *Novascotian*.

"Cringing satellites," snarled the *Patriot*.

"Brawlers! Fanatics!"

"Traitors! Atheists!"

"Jackasses!"

"Boobies!"

It was shortly after this exchange that Joe decided it was time to visit the northern counties. He looked forward with interest to a meeting with the Pictou Reformers.

CHAPTER FIVE
1828-1830

"There never was a country where one man or a dozen men could do so little mischief."

Novascotian, May 1828

A second edition of the *Rambles* came out in the *Novascotian* early in 1829 and in it we read that Mr. Editor Howe arrived in the vicinity of Pictou with humorous misgivings. "The Lord knows whether we may ever live to come out, but here we go merrily in." His words had some basis in fact, for the town was a rough and rowdy spot in that day. In the excitement of a recent election, a man had been killed.

Pictou contained, in the first place, two brands of Presbyterianism always at odds with each other and, in the second, was the home of Nova Scotia's only large group of Reformers, men who openly criticized the government. The leader of these radicals was Doctor Thomas McCulloch, teacher, evangelist and writer of moralistic fiction. Resolved to face the worst at the start, Joe found his way at once to the Academy, where he found both Dr. McCulloch and the *Patriot*'s editor, Jotham Blanchard. The fearsome Blanchard turned out to be a small, lame man in owlish spectacles who smiled and offered his hand to Joe in the friendliest way possible, while Dr. McCulloch greeted him with the Scot's warm hospitality. He showed Joe over the famous Academy, which consisted of one simple wooden building, but housed quite impressive facilities for reading and study. Though it was called an Academy, or high school, it actually taught most college subjects and had a higher standard of teaching than Kings at Windsor. It demanded no religious test from students, as Kings did, though it catered chiefly to the education of Presbyterian ministers. For years Dr. McCulloch had tried to secure a permanent annual grant from the province similar to the one given Kings, but though the Assembly had several times approved his petition, the Council had repeatedly vetoed it.

"Nine members of Council are Anglicans paying respect to a bigoted Bishop," McCulloch said wrathfully, "while they ignore the 80 per cent of our population who are not members of that congregation!"

Joe agreed that this was unfair and said he didn't believe that church denomination should have anything to do with education. But when, out of fairness, he defended the Council, the other said flatly: "It's defective! It's appointed! It holds office for life."

"Any member can be dismissed by the governor for just cause," Joe reminded him.

"My dear Howe," the cultured Scottish voice was heavy with scorn, "when has a member of Council ever been dismissed? Take the Provincial Treasurer. Michael Wallace is one of the most hated men in the province, yet has held that office for nearly thirty years. Jeffrey's been Collector of Customs for nearly the same length of time, and Cogswell's been Provincial Secretary in everything but name for about eighteen years, Sir Rupert George the while enjoying himself in England. And there's Cunard, Collins – but need I go on? You cannot think, surely, these men have performed without fault all that time?"

"No, only that few others in the colony could do better."

"That's not the point, man! Is it proper that *any* group of a dozen men should rule a country without the say of the people in it?"

"But we're a colony, Doctor. The Council must obey the governor and the governor has his instructions from London."

The Principal smiled acidly. "Ah yes, the governor's instructions. Did you ever wonder what they might be, Mr. Howe? I doubt I could make a guess." And here he put on a fair upper class English accent: "Rule firmly, me dear fellow, but not too

47

firmly. We don't want another War of Independence, do we. Take advice from your Council and you can't go wrong. They've held all the offices in the colony for years and know what's good for the country." He resumed his normal accent. "Good for the country, Mr. Howe, or good for themselves? They're over-good, it seems to me, at raising their own salaries."

"As long as they can hand out offices and land grants," said Blanchard, who had been silent up to now, "as long as they can lead governors around by the nose, can make and unmake magistrates and judges' clerks and humble roadmenders, they'll do pretty much as they please – and the country be damned."

"Privilege," Joe said stubbornly, determined not to be bullied, "goes naturally with authority – within reason. As for responsibility to the people, we've got the Assembly for that."

"It's seldom the members of the Assembly do anything but talk," said the Doctor with scorn, "though never against the Council."

"Not true," Joe said instantly. "Surely you heard what the Honourable Tom Haliburton called them not so long ago in the House."

"Aye. 'Twelve dignified old ladies, the one of them in lawn sleeves.' "

Blanchard gave Joe a canny look. "Sometimes if you make enough noise, they'll give you something good to shut you up. Haliburton is after a judgeship."

"If he's made a judge," Joe said with some coldness, for Tom was a friend of his, "it will be because he deserves it. And don't forget Alexander Stewart. He's spoken out with great boldness against the Legislative Council for meeting behind closed doors."

"You'll notice," said McCulloch dryly, "they're still closed."

"It's easy to carp and criticize. How would you reform the Council, if you could?"

"First, I'd separate Executive and Legislative Councils in the sense that no department head could be in both. No man should be able to make the laws and administer them too."

Joe looked doubtful.

"It might be better," suggested Blanchard, "to make the Legislative Council elective like the Lower House."

"That could lead to the formation of political parties," Joe objected.

"But we have parties now," exclaimed the Doctor, "the Reform Party and the Party of Privilege."

And so they argued. Joe met others of the Reform Party and it was the same story.

"Our House of Assembly, Mr. Howe, has no real power at all!"

"By eternally bowing and scraping to the Council to get office, they make a mockery of representative government."

"But they have the power of the purse," he kept insisting. "They can refuse the Revenue Bills."

"Oh aye, the Assembly can stop the supplies all right, and who suffers? Not the councillors. They can pay their own high wages and that's all they care about. Do you think the Twelve mind about the country roads and bridges going to pot for lack of money?"

"I grant you, a few reforms may be needed," began Joe but was interrupted by his old friend Alex McDougall, who had ridden over from Antigonish to see him –

"The whole system needs to be changed."

"We don't want men like Papineau and Mackenzie in Nova Scotia, Sandy," Joe protested, "proposing armed rebellion to correct such minor faults as the closing of the doors of the Legislative Council."

"Who said anything about armed rebellion?" McDougall demanded, "and what is minor about keeping the people in the dark about their own laws? We have no Papineau here that I know of, nor Mackenzie, but I wish we had a moderate like Upper Canada's Robert Baldwin. If his views were listened to in England, we might some day have a responsible government here in Nova Scotia."

Responsible government. Joe turned the words over in his mind cautiously. He knew of course what they meant. It was the next logical step in representative government, the step

England herself had recently taken, making her ministers wholly responsible to the people by always drawing them from the political party having a majority in the House of Commons. He was not yet sure, though, that the principle had any practical meaning for a colony.

On the road again, Joe examined his Pictou experience and knew he had learned from it. Insensibly, he had come round to several of their opinions. Certainly, government salaries were set too high. The Bishop and Chief Justice ought not to be on either Council. He could see reason, too, in separating the legislative body from the executive one, so new Members could be brought in, representing more of the country outside Halifax. But there was no great rush, he thought. Twelve officers of the government, most of whom were very able, decent men, could do little harm to a province with representative government.

After being away from Halifax for nearly two months, Joe looked at his town with fresh perception.

The public buildings, the walls of the new Citadel rising in the west, the elegant homes of the wealthy at north and south ends of Halifax all filled him with pride. In the centre, however, lay the main part of town and here he was shocked at what he saw. Cows and pigs freely roamed the streets, feeding on garbage left in backyards. Drunken men lay about in the lanes, absolutely ignored by the town constables, who stepped over or around them as they went from tavern to tavern collecting licence fees. Surely the town authorities must have noticed these things.

He picked his way along Water Street through mud and squashed cabbages, past the town pump marked "not to be used," and recalled that the sign had been there when he'd left on his travels two months ago. The worst conditions were on the waterfront where privies and cesspools had been allowed to spill over into filthy yards, and the odours of fish market and slaughter-house vied with sewage to make the whole area a stinking horror. Why had the Sanitary Commissioners of the town not done something about these things?

He reached the Green Market at last, where conditions were better, but certainly not perfect. He chose the vegetables Susan Ann had asked him to buy, offering a note in payment. The farmer shook his head.

"That paper stuff's no good."

"Yes it is," Joe said, taken aback for a moment. It was not one of the doubtful notes issued by city merchants for their own convenience, but a proper note of the Halifax Banking Company, better known as Collins' Bank. He told the farmer so.

"Don't matter," the farmer said disgustedly, "the bank won't give hard money for it, just notes and tokens for what they're worth." Hard money was, of course, gold and silver.

Joe had to put back the vegetables and go to another stand, angrily asking himself why Enos Collins and his partners should be allowed to hold on to all the good Spanish dollars and British guineas and hand out paper to their customers. It was too bad there wasn't another bank. What that old pirate and his crew needed was competition. Three other farmers refused Joe's note, demanding silver. A fourth, more ignorant or else more optimistic, did accept it, giving Joe in change one small piece of silver, five or six paper notes and fifty-eight tokens. Joe looked them over in disgust. Nova Scotia's currency was certainly in a bad way. Paper money should never be considered legal, Joe said to himself angrily, unless it could be easily converted to precious metal. The Assembly had tried to put a bill through to this effect not long before, but Council had refused to pass it. Hardly surprising, Joe told himself sourly, since three members of Council were also shareholders of Collins' Bank.

He walked on to the Exchange Coffee House, where he left his vegetables with the porter, and entered the dining-room looking around for his usual companions. He saw Lawrence O'Connor Doyle, foreman of this year's Grand Jury, and joined him. Grand Juries were of course appointed each year from the taxpayers' list, chiefly to make the voice of the ordinary citizen heard in town government. They inquired into indictments before they went to trial, audited the town accounts, and performed other duties having to do with town management. Joe demanded to know what Doyle and his jury meant to do about the currency situation and nuisances like the slaughter-house.

"We try," Doyle said plaintively. "We've been busy enough, the Lord knows. It's taken most of our time so far to make sense of the Treasurer's accounts. They'd make a Philadelphia lawyer wince, so they would. We've got something done about the streets. A few are to be widened and paved."

"Sewers are more important."

"No money. Now don't look at me. What can a poor devil of a juror do but recommend, argue, and put it all in a report to which neither Council nor Assembly pay much heed?"

The friends regarded each other thoughtfully over their cups of coffee. As boys they had played ball in the town streets, cleaner streets then, in a smaller and quieter town. Doyle, an Irishman educated in England, possessed an original mind and an effervescent spirit. He had once ridden horseback up the steps of Province House to behead the stone eagle over the door as a gesture against republicanism. Having recently passed his Bar examinations, he was now trying to settle down as a member of the sedate Uniacke law firm. He was also one of the half-dozen wits who gathered regularly in the back room of Howe's printing shop to compose columns of entertainment for the readers of the *Novascotian*, in something the style of London's Spectator Club. Suddenly Joe wondered if "The Club," as they called it, was not somewhat frivolous. Doyle must have been following out the same line of thought, for he suddenly set down his cup with a crash.

"Joe!" he announced, "the magistrates have too much power! We should start a press campaign for incorporation, and become a city, with a properly elected mayor and aldermen."

Joe made a wry face. "More elections? Haven't we enough spoutings of political nothings and too many broken heads on election days as it is?"

"If you should ever sit on Grand Jury, my lad," said the lawyer, "you'd believe nearly anything would be better than the system we now have."

"Here they are." Joe rose and beckoned to a pair of friends just entering the room. Thomas Chandler Haliburton approached with measured tread, as became a youngish member of the House of Assembly, soon to be a judge. He was often confused with Judge Brenton Halliburton, the member of Council, but was not even related to him. That leading light of Bar and Council, son-in-law to the Bishop of Nova Scotia and father-in-law of Enos Collins, spelled his name with two l's instead of one – "an 'ell of a difference," as the wit of "The Club" was fond of saying.

Nervous, earnest young Will Annand – gentleman-farmer and part-time journalist – loped along, now beside Haliburton, now to the rear, like a small cutter dodging about in the wake of a full-rigged ship. He announced that Dr. Grigor sent his regrets – "He has a full round of patients to see before noon."

"Doyle here thinks the town should be incorporated," Joe said when they were seated. "What about it, Tom?"

The Member for Annapolis raised an imperious hand for the waiter, looked about to see what other notables were present, then gave his attention to the question. "The town is well enough as it is," he pronounced. "When you have incorporation, you have elections, and when you have elections you have parties – the 'Ins' and the 'Outs.' And when you have 'Ins' and 'Outs,' you have two lots of angry people trying to break each other's heads. And the country suffers."

"But surely free elections are better than rule by minority."

"'A horse that's too free'" Haliburton quoted knowingly, "'frets hisself and his rider,' as Sam Slick says, 'and both of 'em lose flesh in the long run.'"

"Who is Sam Slick?" Annand wanted to know.

"You haven't met our Yankee Clockmaker," Haliburton gave Joe a wink. "You will." His famous literary creation, Sam Slick, soon to make T.C. Haliburton's name known on two continents, was nearly ready for serialization in the *Novascotian*.

"Then how are we to get order and decency in this town?"

The decision was promptly handed down. "Let the Grand Jury petition the Governor and Council for an inquiry into the doings of the magistracy in general."

"Petitions and inquiries are a plentiful crop hereabouts," Annand commented, "If they do as much for the town as they have for the province, the Grand Jury may save its breath. Its members are like the assemblymen. They're in office only to help themselves." Realizing too late what he'd said, he glanced from Doyle to Haliburton in some embarrassment. "I didn't mean either of you."

"The Assembly can only do so much," said Haliburton, not at all put out. "If we go beyond our limits, attempt to infringe on the king's prerogative, we only render ourselves ridiculous as well as disloyal. We must occasionally compromise."

"Not I then," exclaimed Doyle. "The fact is, gents, what's wrong with the town is also wrong with the province. Too few in power, and those few entirely irresponsible. They should both be made to account to the people. We must do for Nova Scotia what O'Connell is doing for Ireland." And, seeing Haliburton's smile, he cried "No compromise for yours truly! I've a mind to run for a seat in the House and form a party of my own, a party to speak up for the poor and common like myself." The others laughed, for Doyle's family was one of the wealthiest and most cultured families in town. "Indeed, my lads, I'm in earnest!"

"Of course," said the honourable humorist, "and as long as there's no danger of breaking the connection with Britain, I'm with you."

Joe agreed with Haliburton in principle, but in the light of his recent conversations at Pictou and Yarmouth, he felt for the first time a vague dissatisfaction. Certainly nothing must endanger the connection with England, but might there not be a way to make vital changes without disturbing that relationship? He left the Coffee House with troubled thoughts groping about in his mind.

CHAPTER SIX
1830-1835

"We have here twelve men, who can jeopardize the peace and destroy the revenue of the country."

Novascotian, May 20, 1830

When Joe reached the office of the *Novascotian*, he found Andrew Brown, a former customs clerk of Annapolis waiting to see him.

"I was discharged two months ago without cause," Brown told him, "to make way for a man who's a friend of the local chief magistrate. But that's not why I came to you, Mr. Howe. The fact is, I'm desperate. I must have a job. I've got a wife and six children!"

To be out of work in that day was far more serious than it is now, for there was no unemployment insurance then, no public welfare, and no baby bonus. A man who went without work for long could starve to death or end up, family and all, in the poor-house. By now, Joe Howe was known as a "soft touch" and often his hand went to his pocket to help when he could ill afford such generosity, but here was a case where he could do something without financial strain. He made a list of the names of influential citizens who might be able to help. Probably he needn't go farther than the first name on the list – T.N. Jeffrey, Collector of Customs for the province – who, once he understood Brown's trouble, would find another place for him in the department.

"I wish I could, Howe." Jeffrey, a good-natured man of middle age with whom Joe played racquets occasionally, shrugged an apology. "I make it a point, though, to leave all hiring and firing to my comptroller, John Wallace. However, if a few pounds would help the poor chap –" and his hand went to his pocket.

"It's a job he wants, not charity," Joe said, feeling let down. An open-handed fellow, Jeffrey, but with his salary he could afford to be. Joe knew the comptroller, a son of old Michael Wallace. No use going there.

Next on his list was the lawyer, Johnston, a comparative newcomer to Halifax but already well-known by reputation. Joe had picked him because he was, like Brown, from Annapolis. Also, he was related to Michael Wallace and married to the sister of another Councillor, Dr. Almon, and so might be expected to have influence with Council members. Johnston, moreover, had recently resigned from wealthy St. Paul's on a point of principle to join the more modest Baptist congregation. A man in whom religion and principle managed to meet, thought Joe, ought to recognize an injustice and do something about it.

James Johnston, a handsome middle-aged man of great presence, received Joe graciously and gave his request serious attention. "Yes, I know the man, a very good fellow, and I am sure he is telling the truth." He pulled gently at his chin, his fine eyes thoughtful. "I shall certainly keep him in mind, Mr. Howe. Meanwhile, I hardly know what to suggest. I understand that such places as would be suitable are quite scarce at present. Perhaps if the man had someone of influence to speak for him –" and he gave Joe an expectant look. But that, Joe wanted to tell him, is what I came to you for. He waited a moment, but when the lawyer continued to sit in thoughtful silence, Joe got to his feet.

"Have you tried Alex Stewart?" Johnston asked as they shook hands. Joe hadn't, but it was an idea. Stewart, another lawyer, and one of the younger, more aggressive Members of the House, was spoken of by some as the champion of the people. Stewart's grey eyes flashed when he heard how Brown had lost his job. "That's what we're up against, Howe, patronage and favouritism. It's the same everywhere. All the small towns and villages have their family compacts too, you know, appointed by the one in Halifax, and the society of each revolves around sheriffs, justices and customs clerks. Of course," he added, "there may be something against the man. What about his family?"

"Decent, respectable people as far as I know."

"I meant their background. Politics."

"The family's Loyalist, I believe."

"Good. Religion?"

"Anglican."

"Then where's your problem?" Stewart asked with surprise.

"What does it matter," asked Joe with irritation, "what church he goes to or what his family does, if he's honest and able?"

"It matters," said Stewart grimly. And Joe remembered having heard that Stewart, a Presbyterian, country born and poor, had not had an easy time of it at the start, though now he was doing quite well, both in law and politics. "With the right connections, the man will be all right. Just tell him to be patient."

The disillusioned Joe went to the next name on his list, Enos Collins. Councillor Collins, the town's only banker and a leading merchant of the town since the privateering days of the War of 1812, was said to be North America's richest man.

Surely there would be a place for Brown in one of his businesses. The councillor, a small, thin man of sixty, listened in silence, all the while examining his visitor as if setting a monetary value on him and finding it wasn't much.

"No doubt the man was discharged for good reason," he grunted in reply, "And if he'd saved his money when he had it, he wouldn't be in such straits." He advised Mr. Howe to see the Bishop. Advice cost nothing. And John Inglis, Lord Bishop of Nova Scotia, could only suggest that the man apply to the poor-house, a place nearly as foul as the Bridewell Jail. "So much poverty these days," the Bishop sighed, "usually due to drink or vice, I fear. One wishes to help, but a man in my position has so many calls on his charity."

Joe went away depressed, aware that the Bishop's "position"

brought him in well over two thousand pounds a year, and he was always asking for more.

Very well, he thought, I'll go to the top. In the absence of Governor Sir Peregrine Maitland, Treasurer Michael Wallace was acting administrator of the province. A man of over eighty, face deeply etched by a lifetime of greed and discontent, Wallace was writing in a laboured hand as Joe was shown into his office. He refused to look up until he came to the end of the page. Then he demanded in a sharp tone what was wanted. "Nobody comes here unless they want something."

In a discouraging silence, Joe did his best to make a good case for Brown, but saw before he was half finished that it would be useless.

"Why do you waste my time, Master Howe," Wallace growled impatiently. "I've no time to spend on miserable customs clerks. I have a province to run. Good day to you."

At home, Joe went down his list again and, checking with the *Almanac* to see if he'd overlooked any possibility, he was struck by the fact that the same names appeared over and over again – in government, in business, and in church. Sir Rupert George, for example, was listed as Master of the Rolls, Provincial Secretary, Registrar of the Court of Chancery, of the Court of Marriage and Divorce, of the Court of Errors and Appeals, and of Escheats and Forfeiture! He was also, of course, a member of Council. Then, the son of Judge Brenton Halliburton, President of the Council, was Clerk of the Legislative Council, and the son of Michael Wallace was Customs Comptroller. It was known that another son, now Town Health Officer, looked forward to having the Treasurer's office when his father died. And so it went. Most of these people were related by blood or marriage, belonged to the same church, and were graduates of Kings College.

Down at the bottom of the list was another Kings graduate, Haliburton, spelled-with-one-ell. Joe had put off seeing Tom, reluctant to ask favours of a friend, but now he went to him and told him the story. Haliburton shook his head in wonder.

"What a one you are for trying to take the world on your

shoulders. I could have told you it was a waste of time to see any of those people."

Joe stared at his friend with worried eyes. "So few men, Haliburton, with so much power. Is it fair? Is it really such a good system? Doesn't it allow – even encourage – arrogance and selfishness?"

"My dear Howe," his companion answered with utter conviction, "it's no use asking what is fair. It's what Great Britain wants and what we need – a small but wealthy colonial aristocracy to safeguard the colony from American republicanism." Though a liberal assemblyman, who had at times spoken out in favour of reform, Thomas Chandler Haliburton was essentially a Tory who felt that reckless meddling with the constitution could destroy it. Press reforms gently, he believed, and changes would come in the end. This, up to the present, was what his friend Howe had thought, too.

"Don't worry about Brown," Haliburton said, "I'll see to that little matter. It's all in knowing the right man to see."

So that was done. Andrew Brown would be all right now.

Why then, thought Joe, did he still feel dissatisfied?

It was on a morning near the end of the 1830 Session that Joe Howe's faith in the Council received its final blow. He was in the gallery of the House taking notes, using his grey top-hat as usual as a desk, when the man behind him gave him a nudge and pointed to the gallery exit. Joe went out to find his young pressman, Edward Whelan, waiting in the hall. There was an excited gleam in the young Irishman's eyes, though he began by explaining that it might not be anything much. Though still in his teens, young Whelan was showing every sign of becoming a newspaperman, so Joe gave him a nod of encouragement.

Whelan cast a conspirator's glance over his shoulder – "Casks of brandy are being loaded on carts at Collins' stone building," he whispered, "more than you usually see moving at one time. The draymen seemed in a great hurry and wouldn't say where the brandy was going."

Joe, a little amused at his pressman's excitement, thought

for a moment. This year's Revenue Bill had just gone up to the Legislative Council for approval and contained in it was an increased duty on brandy. This increase was recommended by the Assembly because several years earlier the tax had been mistakenly set too low, and the increase of fourpence per gallon was simply to correct that error. Joe could see no connection between the two things, however, and said so. "But I'm glad you told me," he said. "You might find out if any other merchants are doing the same thing."

He returned to his seat just as a page appeared below with a message from the Legislative Council. It was read aloud. The Council refused to pass the Revenue Bill unless the item on brandy was amended to its previous rate.

In a moment the House was in an uproar. Since 1688, when without violence King James was dethroned, the right of the Commons to the control of the public money had seldom been questioned. Yet here was Nova Scotia's Upper House daring to interfere with the Nova Scotian "Commons" in a money matter. Speaker S.G.W. Archibald left his place and addressed the House with passion. "No principle is more clearly established than that all measures having for their object the taxation of the people must originate in the Lower House. The Upper House has no right in its legislative capacity to make or suggest any alterations."

An eloquent and forceful speaker, Archibald went on to point out that His Majesty's Council objected to the Bill not because it gave too little to His Majesty, but too much! The Assembly had been given power over the public purse precisely in order to balance the power of the Council. "Should we, the people's representatives, impose burdensome or unfair taxes, the people have the ability to put us out at the next election. They have no such control over the Council."

He then reminded the House that since the old Revenue Bill expired that same day, the rejection of the new one would mean that warehouses all over the province would be emptied while the tax was in abeyance. Joe saw now what was happening. In expectation of this very move, wily old Enos Collins had started moving his brandy out to customers, either to sell at the lower rate existing, or duty free if the Assembly refused to consider changing it. "If this Bill is allowed to be amended," Archibald warned, "it will be a dangerous precedent. Once the House submits to encroachment on the people's rights, it will become a shadow and a name."

When it came to a vote, the majority refused to consider altering the Bill. The Council refused again to pass it, and Acting Administrator Michael Wallace promptly dissolved the House. Other merchants now saw their chance to sell to advantage while the Revenue Bill was inoperative, and did so. Twenty-five thousand dollars in revenue was suddenly lost to the people of Nova Scotia, and Joe's lingering respect for the Council vanished forever. All that money lost to Nova Scotia, just so a few brandy merchants could use their privileged position to make a slightly larger profit! The Council had acted in a way to benefit themselves and hurt the province, and this Joe could not excuse.

On the governor's return, a writ was issued for the election of a new Assembly, and Joe threw all the influence of the *Novascotian* on the side of the Members who had refused to amend the Bill. Almost every one was returned.

"You see?" cried the *Novascotian* in triumph, "the House of Assembly *does* have power, when public opinion is shown to be firmly behind the majority." Members of Council would never dare again, he said, to put its own interests ahead of the country's. A second incident, however, in the next Session, showed how wrong Joe was on both counts. It had to do with Nova Scotia's currency.

The only bank up to this time was Collins' Bank, and at that time four of its directors were members of His Majesty's Council. When in this year, 1831, a group of Halifax merchants applied to open another, the Bill of Incorporation went automatically to the Legislative Council for approval, and this was the equivalent of putting it before the directors of the other bank! Master Collins and his partners, not wanting competition, yet not caring to upset the country by simply turning the Bill down, sent it back to the Lower House demanding outrageous amendments. The worst was the one which said the new bank must always have sufficient gold and silver on hand to cover the paper money it issued.

Joe, after his own sad currency experience, was all for this rule, but pointed out in the *Novascotian* that the same rule should apply to Collins' Bank. The applicants for the second bank agreed. "One rule for Collins, another for us? Ridiculous!" But Council persisted in demanding the amendments.

When it became clear that the Assembly, yielding to pressure behind the scenes, was willing to compromise, Joe was aghast. The Bank of Nova Scotia would be incorporated, it was agreed, but neither bank would be required to redeem its notes in metal. This was a most shameful solution, for it meant that Nova Scotia would still have to juggle with dubious notes and tokens and, if the banks should ever fail, only the depositors would suffer. Once again His Majesty's Council had acted to benefit its members without regard for the country.

What upset Joe as well was the fact that no Member of the Assembly, not his admired S.G.W. Archibald, not new Member Jotham Blanchard of Pictou, not even champion-of-the-people Stewart would move that *both* banks be required to safeguard the people's money.

Joe's love affair with the Assembly, too, was over. He had become a Reformer.

This did not mean that he would run for election to the Assembly. He believed he could do more for his province by influencing public opinion through the pages of his paper, for the *Novascotian* was now one of the most influential and well read papers, not only in the Maritimes, but in all British North America. It printed news from Europe and the United States as well as the provinces, and the doings of all the various legislatures were carefully reported and commented on. When, for example, word came that the Reform Bill had passed in Britain's parliament, Joe gave it full coverage. He and young Whelan stayed late one evening to set up the story on the press.

"We've come a long way," Whelan said, swabbing vigorously at the ink-stained plates, "since the ancient Greeks first allowed their citizens to be heard in the marketplace."

"It was the English who invented representative government though," Joe said, "The Greek method of letting men speak individually was good, but it wouldn't work in anything larger than a city. It wasn't until the reign of Edward First that the English saw the need for representatives to speak for the people at large and won the right to elect an assembly."

"How *did* they win it, Mr. Howe?"

"I'll tell you," Joe said with a laugh. "One day the king was, as usual, in need of money and he called on all the English counties to send delegates of their choice to report on how much tax they could raise for him in each district. The delegates did so, but made sure their petitions were all answered before they would deal with money matters. They also made it clear that, since they were raising the money, they must have some say in the spending of it." Young Whelan smiled with pleasure. "And that's how the public purse came under the control of the people, Whelan, and how the House of Commons was born. By 1688, when Lords and Commons together threw out James the First and put William of Orange on the throne, it was very clear that power had moved from king to parliament."

"When did Britain's present cabinet government come into effect sir?"

"I can't give you a date for that, I'm afraid." Joe smiled at the young man's surprise. "It just grew. Like a rose or a carrot," he added nostalgically. "As my sister once explained it to me, government grows best when it grows slowly, step by step. Violent revolutions nearly always do as much harm as good. Britain's present form of ministerial government for instance didn't even need an act of parliament to bring it into being. It just slowly and gradually became the custom for a government to resign when its party lost the majority in parliament. That's the British way, you see, and that's why this Reform Bill is so important. Not only did it reform the electoral system of Britain, so in future all men can vote, it marked the full maturity of cabinet government."

"That's what we should have in Nova Scotia," Whelan said energetically. Seeing Joe's dubious expression, he looked disappointed. "But why not, sir?"

"I'm not sure that cabinet government would suit a colony.

Not yet anyway. It would mean political parties which, in a lusty young country like ours, could lead to a bitter fight for power. In the fighting, the country's needs might be forgotten. There must be a better way."

"We *ought* to fight," Whelan said fiercely. "We can't let the Council go on forever doing just as its members please."

"It has too much power," Joe agreed. "The trouble is, its members are appointed for life. Governors come and go, Members of the Assembly change, but the councillors go on forever. Dying, they hand the reins to sons or brothers. If Britain would forbid this sort of thing, the Twelve's power might be broken. But," he added briskly, "there's more than one way to fight, Whelan. Education is an excellent way, and that's where we come in. Now let's get to work and we'll have this story off the press by midnight."

There were those in Halifax who considered the Reform Bill in a different light. In his study that evening, Enos Collins was reading a letter from his father-in-law, Brenton Halliburton, in London at that moment doing all he could to ensure his appointment as Chief Justice when the present holder of it died. "The people in this country have really gone mad for reform," he wrote, "and England's established institutions are being sacrificed to the need to yield to the popular voice."

Collins picked up his quill pen. "Do not give in on anything to do with Nova Scotia," he warned his father-in-law, "So sure as you do, away goes all the influence of His Majesty's Council."

From 1829 to 1832, Joe had been hearing and finally answering to the trumpet call for reform. His conversion had begun with his visits to Yarmouth and Pictou, had finished with the brandy and currency battles. Now came his appointment to Grand Jury duty. He hailed the opportunity with delight. "I intend to transform a lukewarm cluster of citizens into a devoted band of civic reformers," he told Susan Ann, and appeared at the first meeting full of energy and determination.

In the Minutes of January, his name appears at the tail end of a committee investigating the scarcity of copper coin. By

March, it heads the list of several committees, one requesting that the Assembly pass an act prohibiting the slaughter of cattle within the town limits. The rider to it is in Joe's straightforward style: "This evil has been complained of before and nothing has been done about it." At once the magistrates, who until then had shown little interest in Grand Jury proceedings, were up in arms. They demanded the removal of the last clause. Otherwise, they said, it would look as though they were being censured, and to Joe's disgust, the clause was struck out. It was the Assembly spirit all over again.

"It's only a matter of time, Howe," Dr. William Grigor prophesied, "before some vessel brings the European cholera to Halifax, and when it does, that filthy slaughter-house will certainly spread the disease."

Joe thought with a shiver of his young family. "We need a new hospital too."

"Also a new poor-house and a new jail," Grigor declared grimly. "For that matter, we need a whole new Board of Health, in spite of what Jeffrey said." Customs Collector Jeffrey had recently complimented the central and local boards of health on their "vigour and vigilance." "Can't you people on the Grand Jury do something?"

"We can try," said Joe, "but it's like trying to move a whale!"

Joe worked so hard to make the whale move, he laid himself open to an infection, probably typhus, and for a short time was so ill Dr. Grigor despaired of his life. By the time Joe recovered, his service with the Grand Jury was over and little had been accomplished after all. The best they had been able to do was to refuse to levy any assessment for that year, saying that if back taxes were collected from those well able to pay, there would be plenty of money to run the town.

That summer the province felt the pinch of hard times, and following two bad harvests in a row, several bankruptcies occurred in Halifax. Yet this year a new and higher scale of salaries was proposed by the Council's supporters in the Assembly for the already overpaid governor and judges. "Every time we protest," the Grand Jury said indignantly, "they raise their own pay."

Joe, still weak from his illness, but with the spectre of bank-ruptcy haunting him, as it did others, had to put aside politics for a time and go on the road again. This trip was no leisurely ramble. Here are excerpts from his letters to Susan Ann:

Truro (after a ride of 115 miles on horseback): "For the first time since I left home, I can trace in my feelings and looks some indication of returning health." *Antigonish*: "My steed got mired and pitched me first upon his neck and then upon my back. I escaped however without being hurt." He sent his wife £5 for fear it should be needed, but warned her not to spend or pay a shilling of it if she could help it. *Guysborough*: "I have fared so badly that I shall be under the painful necessity of going further. I start tomorrow in the packet for Arichat. In Cape Breton I have some £45 due me, and if I get even half of it, it will be a week well spent." *Pictou*: "I wish from my heart I was with you and money in my pocket. Tell Edward to be a good boy. Make him write me a letter." He sent maple sugar to all the children and wished he were at home having a frolic with them on the sofa.

Susan Ann wrote back, alarming him with the news that the cholera had come to Halifax. The new Dalhousie college had been turned into an infirmary and all the doctors were rushed off their feet. The Rifle Brigade had lost twenty-nine men. Joe thought of his wife, of the toddlers Ellen and Mary, of Edward, and especially the baby, Joseph. He turned homeward, trav-elling as hard and as fast as he could.

His road took him through a Micmac settlement and he spared time to look up an old friend, Chief Peters, to deliver a gift of tobacco. He was saddened to hear that the old man had died and was shocked to see that the family lived mostly on the bounty of Indian neighbours little better off than themselves. These neglected native people, thought Joe indignantly, were a reproach to their white rulers.

Again, riding through Preston, a community of black peo-ple, mainly refugees from the States after the War of 1812, he saw the same thing, an apathetic minority ignored by the authorities. His mind, as he rode along, wrestled with ways to provoke the government into helping these people, but when he turned into the Kempt Road at last and saw the first Halifax houses appear in the distance, his thoughts all leapt ahead to his own family.

The streets were quiet, ominously so, and it was a Saturday too. The Green Market was closed tight. Country folk would not risk bringing produce to the cholera-stricken town. Besides, most of their well-to-do customers would have gone to their country farms to live until the disease ran its course.

Urging his tired mare on faster, Joe finally reached home, to find all safe and well, for which blessing he heartily thanked God.

"They say the epidemic is losing strength with the cold weather," Susan Ann told him. "Did you know that forty deaths occurred in that overcrowded poor-house?" Joe blushed with shame. If his Grand Jury had worked harder to get a new poor-house, perhaps many of those poor souls would have lived.

She told him too that the 1834 Grand Jury was a fighting one, like the one he had been on, and that his friend James Leishman was foreman. They were trying to uncover the misdeeds of the present Bridewell Commissioner, one Magistrate Roche, a grain dealer, who was thought to be making a good thing out of the jail. Joe was not surprised to receive a visit from Leishman early next morning. "Roche sells the jail all its flour," Leishman told him, "much of it sour and short weight, but at top prices. He uses the prisoners as his personal servants. One makes boots for him and his family. Another made him a bath, and still another a birdcage. He keeps his horse in the jail woodshed instead of his own and stores his hay in the jail guardhouse. These are small things, perhaps, but they show how the wind blows. We finally got the Sessions to hold an inquiry." Leishman gave an angry shrug "You can imagine the good it did. The magistrates asked only the questions which would bring out the right answers and the worthy Roche was cleared of all blame."

Joe's mind rushed back twenty-five years to that day in the Bridewell with his father. He saw Matt the Lamplighter as vividly as if the old man stood before him with the heavy collar around his neck. He remembered how he had vowed to make the jailors and magistrates do their duty. And so far he had done nothing.

Leishman, he knew, hadn't come for a gossip. "What do you want from me?"

"Print the Grand Jury's Annual Report when it's ready."

"Is that all?" Joe felt a sense of reprieve. The reports were always printed, though no one seemed to pay them much attention.

"This time," Leishman said grimly, "we'll hand it with a memorial to the Governor the minute he arrives at Halifax, before the Council can get hold of him."

If the new Governor, Sir Colin Campbell, acted on the Jury's recommendations, it would postpone the need for Joe Howe to decide how far he personally dared go. He could not dodge commitment forever, but he must be sure that if he took risks – risks to his family or his business – they would have worthwhile results. He was not optimistic about memorials; they had been tried before. The magistrate always had friends on the Council who would intervene with the governor, or they would bring pressure to bear on the committee, if and when it was formed, and everything would be glossed over as usual.

Something more was needed – something striking. Something to wake up the people as well as the governor. He had seen already how the press could force public action and how the force of public opinion affected the Members of the Assembly. Yet when the "something more" turned up in his office one morning late in 1834, Joe was not at all certain he wanted anything to do with it. It consisted of two letters written by his friend, George Thompson, calling for action against the town government. The first letter was mild and Joe published it without much concern. Over the second, he hesitated. It was certainly startling. It flatly accused the magistrates and police of *stealing* by one strategem or another, over the past thirty years, more than thirty thousand pounds! The magistrates could not afford to ignore this accusation and they would look for a scapegoat. Not necessarily the writer of the letters. More likely that gadfly, the *Novascotian*. Or its editor!

He had others to think of, besides himself. Father, John, and Mother's son, Joseph Austen, were all magistrates. Father, particularly, did not deserve to share the blame that was bound to fall on all the town officials. There was the paper. If it offended men in high places, it would lose advertising and circulation, possibly go bankrupt. Finally, there was his family, who could suffer for years as a result of any or all these eventualities.

There were still others to consider. There were the people who had died in the cholera epidemic. There were the blacks and the Indians, the inmates of jail and poor-house, and even the memory of old Matt the Lamplighter.

If the *Novascotian* were ever to do anything worthwhile for Nova Scotia, it must start soon. Risks must be taken, first or last. Joe read the letter again. It was time the people were protected from men like Roche! It was the duty of an honest editor to publish and risk the consequences! He called his foreman and gave him the letter.

"Print it."

Now there was no turning back.

At first it seemed that this letter too would be ignored. Then, early in February 1835, Joe received a visit from Attorney General S.G.W. Archibald who, half apologetically, handed him an indictment for criminal libel.

Though he had known this could happen, Joe could not at first make sense of the words in the document: "Joseph Howe, printer, being a wicked, seditious and ill-disposed person ... of a most wicked and malicious temper ... has published a certain libel with a view to injure and degrade ..." He, Joe Howe, seditious and ill-disposed to authority? It was ludicrous. The prospect of being tried for libel, however, was no laughing matter.

It was one thing to consider an indictment as a remote possibility, quite another to be faced with it in the present. Into his mind rushed words addressed to Will Wilkie by the judge fifteen years before:

"Two years in the Bridewell at hard labour!"

CHAPTER SEVEN
1835

"The most negligent and imbecile body that ever mismanaged a people's affairs."

Libel Defense, March 1835

Resolutely, Joe put his fears aside and went looking for a lawyer. He went to half a dozen. Each said he had no case – the truth was no defence in libel.

"They won't let you bring evidence, you see, or call witnesses," one of them said. "Once you admit you published the letter, you're as good as convicted. Your one hope is to name the author." But this Joe would not consider.

Another offered to get him off with a light sentence.

"Thanks just the same," said Joe wryly.

Still another grinned at his plight. "Sooner have a go yourself? Well, you know what they say –"

Before the words could be uttered Joe finished the quotation. "'The man who defends himself has a fool for a client'; yes, I know."

Even his close friends couldn't help. "It's no use deceiving you Howe," Tom Haliburton said grimly. He was now a judge of the court of Common Pleas and unable, if he wished, to take Joe's case. "There's no doubt the letter is a libel."

"From a legal standpoint, he means," said Doyle, his Irish face serious for once. "I'm afraid you must apologize to the Sessions. Then they may drop the case."

"Unthinkable!" Joe said.

"They'll make an example of you" Annand fretted. "They'll bury you under that bill of indictment."

"They'll find me a lively corpse."

"Don't decide in a hurry," Haliburton warned him. "You know nothing of the law, nor of how to appeal to a jury. If you must fight, let one of your professional friends help you."

If Doyle and Haliburton both thought there was no defence, of what use was a lawyer? "Thanks, but I think something can be done, and I can do it better alone. You might lend me some of your lawbooks." They put all they had at his disposal. "If only Joe's knowledge of the law," they said to each other with deep foreboding, "equalled his nerve."

That same evening, Susan Ann sat trying to sew as she listened to her husband's footsteps pacing back and forth overhead. When at last he came down, she knew by the set of his shoulders, the sparkle in his eye, that he meant to fight.

"What can I do to help, Joseph?"

He hugged her. "Pray." His natural optimism was back, though. "I think I'll have a better chance than a lawyer. The Court is bound to allow an amateur some leeway."

He went off in the morning to arrange for someone to run the paper for a fortnight, and was barely able to get down the passage to his office for the crowd there, all offering help and information. Most had some complaint of their own against the magistrates and several said they would willingly testify. Joe had to explain that he was not allowed to use witnesses. By the law of that time, as in the Wilkie case, he could not defend himself by proving the truth of what he had published. The fact that he had published something which could damage the reputation of a public man was sufficient to convict him. That was the bad part; the good thing was that although Chief Justice Brenton Halliburton would preside over the bench of judges, there would be a jury and it was those twelve men who would decide the verdict. He, the accused, would be allowed to defend himself if he could, but how was he to bring out the facts without witnesses and without appearing to defy the libel law?

He spent the two weeks before the trial reading law and looking up British precedents. In the end, he had no time to write out a speech, only plan its rough shape and memorize the first two paragraphs. He came down that last evening, stretching cramped muscles.

"Put on something warm, Susie, and come for a walk."

The two set out briskly in the chill March air, down Pleasant Street to the old Kissing Bridge, then more slowly up the hill to Fort Massey. From there they could look down on the dark patch that was Halifax town, dimly lit by flickering lights. Other lights, ships' lights, showed here and there on the paler expanse of the Harbour with Dartmouth a dark line beyond. They could hear the Crier calling the time: "Ten o'clock and all's well."

"If only I were a better, more practised speaker." He had the habit of stammering when he was nervous.

"They tell me you spoke very well at the Institute last summer." She meant the Mechanics' Institute, a sort of nineteenth-century adult education group to which Joe had lectured on several occasions. But it was not the same. So much hung on what happened tomorrow – his career, his reputation, even his freedom. Susan Ann knew as well as he that he was throwing into the scales all they both held most dear, yet spoke no word of reproach. Wilkie was a name never spoken between them.

"I know what I want to say," he told her, "if only I can say it without breaking down. Surely if I put the whole case before them as I see it, if they're fair and rational men they must acquit me."

She said to him what he had so often said to her.

"All will be well, dear."

He squeezed her hand, tucked it under his arm, and they turned homeward.

The great mass of people attending the trial soon made the chilly courtroom of Province House as warm as a furnace. Joe, gazing about him, saw many faces he knew. All his friends were there who could get a seat, including Grigor and Leishman and Doyle. Doyle, in his old green cutaway coat, dusty as always, sent him a beaming, confident smile. Susan Ann was a rock of comfort beside Father in the front row. A good many lawyers were present, no doubt waiting to see him make a fool of himself. Even a few of the magistrates had shown up, William Roche for one. Joe marvelled. Surely he must know that even if Joe were convicted, he himself could not go out of court with his reputation intact. Perhaps he counted on self-interest to keep the printer's tongue silent.

On the dais with the other judges sat the new Chief Justice Halliburton, his slight form impressive in wig and gown. Joe wondered if Halliburton had read a recent piece in the *Novascotian* which said flatly that a Chief Justice should not be a member of Council or meddle in politics. As in the Wilkie trial, S.G.W. Archibald was chief prosecutor, with James Gray assisting. Joe had been outspoken lately about Archibald's waverings in the House, but that should mean little one way or the other. He would do his duty.

A special jury had been called. Five of them had served with Joe on the 1832 Grand Jury and would no doubt be sympathetic. Five others were near relatives of the magistrates his paper had attacked. He could hardly hope for a unanimous verdict.

When all were sworn in and the foreman appointed, Gray opened the case for the Crown. "This indictment states that on the first of January a certain libel was published in the *Novascotian* with a view to injure and degrade and bring into disrepute the magistrates of the town of Halifax." He read the offending letter and Joe's fears returned in full force. How had he ever supposed he could prevail against this array of legal talent? He knew a moment of sheer panic in which he distinctly saw himself breaking stones in the yard of the Bridewell.

He forced himself to remain calm, to listen.

"It is for you to say whether or not the matter charged is of a libellous nature," Gray told the jury, "as well as to say who is the publisher and what his intent."

Joe wrote down the word "intent."

Gray then asked the jury to note that not one person but a whole group had been injured – all the magistrates who had served in the past thirty years – and surely they could not all have been at fault. Joe wrote down "neglect."

"There is no doubt," Gray said in conclusion, gazing over the courtroom, "that the prosecution here are contending against the popular side of the question, but juries in Halifax have always done justice between parties." His charge had taken less than an hour.

The name "Hugh Blackadar" was called to establish publication, but there was no reply. Presumably Blackadar was unwilling to testify against a fellow editor. Joe rose then and said he was the proprietor of the *Novascotian* and admitted the letter in question had appeared in that paper with his knowledge on the first of January. The Chief Justice looked down on him as if from an immense distance.

"How does the defendant plead?"

"Not guilty, My Lord."

"I understand you wish to make your own plea to the jury."

"If you please, My Lord."

"Proceed."

As Joe turned from the Bench to the jury, a hush fell over the room.

"My Lords and gentlemen –" To his alarm he heard his voice quaver, and saw the anxious look in his wife's eyes. He smiled at her, then took a long deliberate breath. "I entreat you to believe," he said firmly, "that no ostentatious desire for display has induced me to undertake the labour and responsibility of this defence." He told them he had planned to engage a lawyer but later thought that he himself, by making a simple appeal to truth and justice, might do better.

He had conquered the stammer so far, thank God. With a glance at the court reporter, to make sure he was not speaking too quickly, he continued: "I have felt, besides, that if the press is to be subjected to a series of persecutions like this, it is indispensable to the safety of those who conduct it, that they should learn to defend themselves." It was the end of what he had memorized.

He gathered up his notes, stated what would be his defence: "If, in resisting a burglar, I knock my friend upon the head, I cannot be convicted of crime; and if, in opposing a public robber, I utterly destroy his reputation, the jury try me by motive, not by the severity of the infliction." Several lawyers shook their heads in grave disapproval, but Doyle cheered silently "Go it, Joe!" his broad face redder than usual from the heat and excitement.

"With nearly all of the individuals assailed, I have been on friendly terms for years ..." With a part of his mind he was seeing ahead. At the same time, he was sharply aware of the crowd and of the Bench and jury and of his own amazing position in the dock. He made his voice stern: "As magistrates, I know them, as you know them, to be the most negligent and imbecile, if not the most reprehensible, body that ever mismanaged a people's affairs."

Applause broke out and the Chief Justice rapped for order.

Then Joe got down to business. He described the unequal way in which taxes were levied, how clerks and magistrates foreclosed on the poor and let others go who could well afford to pay. He described the slovenly way in which accounts were kept. "In these charges of neglect, I include *all* the magistrates. The law makes a looker-on at a felony a partner in the crime."

When the noon hour came, Joe was telling of visits to the Bridewell with his father. He described with emotion the woman in the stocks and the old man with the cruel collar about his neck. An elderly gentleman in the jury box shed tears.

Then he brought them back to the present, reminding them of the Grand Jury's charges against Commissioner Roche. People stole glances at the Commissioner, who smiled his contempt. The colour rose to his cheeks, however, when Joe described how he was like the ruler in Scripture who said to one go and he goeth and to another do this and he doeth it. "When this man and his family walked abroad, their feet were protected by the county. When they were disposed to enjoy the luxury of the bath, the county furnished the tubs, and even the melody of Miss Roche's canary was breathed through cages manufactured at the public's expense." There was growing pleasure at the magistrate's discomfiture. "If you send me there, I shall be compelled to print him a newspaper for nothing, and then the list of his luxuries will be pretty complete."

The laughter would not be hushed until Chief Justice Halli-

75

burton delivered a warning: "The public may laugh at the defendant's witticisms in moderation, but those who laugh to excess will be charged with contempt and removed from the courtroom."

Joe dealt next with the charge of sedition by quoting an article he had published a few years earlier entitled *Loyalty to the Crown*. "While I sat in my office penning these passages some of their worships were plundering the poor. If His Majesty sat on that Bench, he would tell them that he who robs the subject makes war on the King. He would tell them *they* were the rebels, and that against them and not against me, this bill of indictment should have been filed."

He kept reminding them that, though he knew he was not allowed to present facts as proof, he understood it was his duty to show that, when he published the letter in question, he did not do it to make a breach of peace, but to preserve it. He insisted on his good *intention*. In this way, he got round the rule of law and managed to bring out the truth just the same.

The clock moved on to four. The crowd stayed on, not missing a word. Joe could hardly believe he'd been speaking for more than six hours, mostly without notes. Gathering his strength for a final assault, he let his ragged voice deepen and carry to every corner of the room –

"Will you, my countrymen," he asked with passion, "permit the sacred fires of liberty, brought by our fathers from the venerable temples of Britain, to be quenched and trodden out on the simple altars they have raised? Your verdict will be the most important in its consequences ever delivered before this tribunal, and I conjure you to judge me by the principles of English law, and to leave an unshackled press as a legacy to your children."

He concluded by thanking the Court for its patience and sat down. There was a moment of silence, then a roar of applause. Attorney-General Archibald, rising to speak, was stopped by the Chief Justice who said that, as the hour was late and the jury confined so long, it would be best to adjourn until the next day. "Unfair," a voice shouted, "it's giving the other side extra time" and there was an outburst of agreement and protest which broke off when Joe rose again. He said he did not wish to shut out anything that could shake his statement and the foreman said the jurymen were willing to stay; but at this point the crowd and the heat and confusion became too much for the Bench who sternly ruled that the Court adjourn.

Exchanging a glance with his wife, Joe spoke to the sheriff who eased him out ahead of the crowd. He ran down the steps, crossed the road and let himself into his own house. Closing the door, he leaned against it, let tears roll unchecked down his cheeks. The reaction was enormous and natural. He had been under tremendous strain for six hours and a quarter. He felt exalted and at the same time, humble. The tears kept coming.

Hearing his wife's voice outside, he moved from the door, heard her plead with someone to go away. "Let him have his supper. Come afterwards."

A moment later the latch lifted and she came in, saw him standing there and paused, searching his face with wonder. Then she went into his arms. After a while, he found his voice. "It was" – he groped vainly for a word and fell back on understatement – "all right. Wasn't it." She nodded. "The Lord must have helped. How else could I have spoken like that?" He added, with wonder, "I never stammered once."

"You held us all in the palm of your hand," she said. "You mesmerized us."

He was amazed. "Was that it? Can one have such power without knowing it?"

She came down to earth and brought him with her. "Of course not. You were simply strong in your beliefs, Joseph, and found the words to make us believe too."

Things fell into proportion. "You're right, Susan. To speak the truth – and feel it – that's what convinces. But the question is," he added with a rueful grin, "will the spell stay on overnight? The judge will be sure to bring the jury up to the mark."

"You've done all you can," she said. "Worry won't help. Come now and see what Hannah's got for our supper."

The crowd next morning was larger than ever, spilling out of Province House into the street. They were a cheerful lot, joking and shuffling their feet to keep warm, but they seemed watchful too, as if they knew that what was happening inside concerned them all. In the courtroom, at exactly ten o'clock, Attorney General Archibald rose, and Joe braced himself. Here was the man who so often in the House had held him in thrall with his eloquence.

"In calling your attention to this case," Archibald began, "I will endeavour to divest it of the amazing importance which has been thrown around it, and bring it down to those plain rules of law by which alone it must be decided." In a pleasant, passionless tone, he urged the jury to dismiss all emotion, since nothing but the cool operation of the mind, influenced by evidence, and the plain principles of common law, could be effectual in keeping the peace. "If the peace of society is broken, who is to repair it? Not the press. That is not the tribunal."

He explained the law of libel and described its dangers. He declared that the defendant's charges against the magistrates were statements without proof. He closed his speech with a warning: "Be careful that your verdict be not the occasion of greater mischief, that you do not open the floodgates of libelling."

It remained now for His Lordship to charge the jury.

Regarding the twelve men severely over his spectacles, Judge Brenton Halliburton told the Court that the magistrates were not the Accused. The jury stared back without expression. "Your verdict," insisted the Chief Justice, "will not condemn or acquit them. It is not in the columns of a newspaper that they are to be tried and condemned." According to the law, the Judge's summing-up was fair. He said quite plainly that the paper was a libel, Mr. Howe had published it, and there was no legal escape.

Yet after only ten minutes the jury returned and the verdict was unanimous: "We find the defendant 'not guilty'."

It was impossible for the Bench to keep order. The excitement spread into the corridor, down the broad steps and out into Granville Street, and when Joe emerged the crowd swept down on him, shook his hand, hugged him, clapped him on the back, and some cried. Then, hoisting him on their shoul-

Susan Ann Howe (1807-1890) wife of Joe Howe.

ders, they bore him through the cheering, laughing crowd to his front door.

He pleaded to be let down from his insecure perch and made a short speech of thanks, urging them to keep the peace. "And be sure," he said, "to teach your children the names of the twelve men who have just established the freedom of the press." Here, Joe was a bit carried away. He must have known, if he thought about it, that the law can be changed only by a statute of parliament, not by the verdict of a jury. It would be another eight years before defendants could, in the public interest, use truth as a defence in libel. The jury had not established the freedom of the press, nor had they handed down a verdict of Joe's innocence. What they had done, swayed by his courage and eloquence, was deliver a virtual verdict of guilty against the magistracy, and by implication, against the governor and Council who had appointed them. However, this fact was temporarily overlooked in the joyful excitement.

Bands played and all the sleds in town turned out that night with banners and bells. All the next day, too, people came to call and congratulate Howe on his victory. It was enough to go to a man's head. Perhaps it did, a little.

"The trial," he wrote his sister, who no doubt anxiously awaited word of its outcome, "has been a tremendous triumph. For six hours and a quarter I defended myself and scourged my persecutors, in a style that of course I was too busy to judge of, but which startled and astonished the multitude, who devoured every word like manna." One may read egotism in this letter, but remember he was writing to the sister who knew him as well as he knew himself and he could say what he really felt. And Joe Howe was a man who always made the most of his triumphs and pleasures, which was perhaps wise, since he would have plenty of failure and pain to endure in his life as well.

The Howe family had its private celebration. Old John Howe, a little muddled these days, had only vaguely followed the proceedings, but he knew his Joseph had won. "I knew you'd thrash them," he said contentedly, sipping his glass of wine. "I thought they had better let you alone."

He added that he hoped Joseph was now finished with politics and would settle down to more peaceful pursuits. A few months later, the good old man died in his sleep, without knowing that his favourite son was planning to run as Reform candidate for a seat in the House of Assembly.

CHAPTER EIGHT
1836-1837

*"I doubt whether it [Party Government]
would work well here."*

Novascotian, February 1837

During his seven years in the gallery, Joe had many times
wished he was down in the arena. Impatient with errors and
faintness of heart, he had in imagination taken part in the
debates and led Members in the way they should go. Yet
whenever others – Doyle, for one, now member for Arichat –
had suggested he become a candidate, Joe had always laughed.
"What, me run against all you clever lawyers and trained
speakers? No thanks!"

But that was before the trial.

Before the trial, Nova Scotia had known him only as Mr.
Editor or "young Howe." After it, he was the Nova Scotian
hero who had revealed the evils of town government and
caused half a dozen magistrates to resign. Before it, Joe had
been a stammering, indifferent speaker. After it, he knew he
could, when his heart was in it, sway men with words.

"If I meet a man in the forest," he wrote Susan Ann on his
first trip after the trial, "or standing in a shed out of the rain, I
have only to say my name and at once they want to shake
hands with me. They ask about the trial and about the banks
and offer to do me any little service in their power. Please God,
if I ever get my hands a little free, I will endeavour to do something much more worthy of all this than anything I have done
yet."

He now accepted the need for some sort of "responsible" government, but had as yet no clear idea what form it should take. He feared party conflict as much as ever and was emphatic that rebellion was not the answer. When a Canadian Reformer named Chapman suggested the Nova Scotians join other British Americans in a demonstration against the family compacts, Joe replied bluntly that he suspected the Canadians of having armed revolt in mind, and Nova Scotia wanted none of that. If there was any joining to be done, he thought it ought to be with the Colonial Reformers of England, men in the British parliament who were openly sympathetic to the needs of the colonies and who could help them in peaceful and constitutional ways.

For the moment, he had decided, what was most needed was a majority of Reformers in the House of Assembly, and someone in it to provide leadership. Some spirit must be injected into the Members, some sort of responsible form of government worked out, and who could do these things better than he? He must, therefore, get himself elected. There was vanity in this reasoning, but no man ever did anything worthwhile without having confidence in himself.

Now was the time, if ever. His paper was picking up financially as its circulation grew. Most of his debts were paid. Though personally extravagant – he would tip a boy half a crown for holding his horse just to enjoy the pleasure and surprise in the child's face – yet he was careful in business matters and conscientious about paying what he owed. Here was his mother's influence showing. He saw the risks. Any man who opposed the establishment would make enemies, but he had never been afraid of enemies.

He gave his sister Jane yet another reason for going into active politics: "As I got no regular education, I have always held to the wisdom of picking it up as we go along. Circumstances teach one better than books, and to learn to reason and think and act with clearness and energy, a man should put himself into situations that compel him to do all these as often as possible."

Tom Haliburton, though a Member himself, did not encour-

William Annand (1808-1887) journalist, early reformer, and a leading anti-Confederate.

age Joe to run. He thought the *Novascotian* could no longer be considered independent if its editor was an active Reformer, and in consequence he and his paper would suffer. "Consider well," he wrote from his home in Windsor, "cipher like Slick [the Clockmaker]. Set down the advantages on one side – it will make a deuced small column – and put the disadvantages on the other. Then strike a balance. ... If you do offer, I have no fears for you. You are an old navigator, though you do crack on sail like the devil sometimes."

Susan Ann was another shaken by doubts. She had none of his driving urge to change things and was happy with her home and her children. She enjoyed music and needlework, and yearned for a family security which so far had eluded the Joe Howes. She had seen enough to know that men in public life had little time for home and children and, if they were honest and foolishly generous like her husband, precious little financial security. But after seven years of marriage she knew his restless searching mind, his incredible energy, his small vanities and huge ambitions.

Naturally Joe talked it over with her, for they had been a team from the start. It was not usual in that age for a man to consult his wife about so important a matter as his career. Susan Ann was aware of this and was defeated at the start by his generosity. She agreed that he must do what he thought right, and she would help him as much as she could.

So in the summer of 1836, Joe Howe and Will Annand announced themselves as Reform candidates for Halifax County, and shortly after, set out on their first election campaign.

There were then, of course, no organized parties. A candidate, if he favoured Reform, might be known as a Reformer, or, if he wanted to keep things as they were, as a Tory. But it did not mean, as it does today, that if he won he would go into power on the government side and sit in a Cabinet or on a back bench; nor that, if he lost, he would form part of the Opposition. A Reformer like Howe simply ran against another man for a seat in the House where, in a small but constitutional way (that is, according to the rules of parliament) he might act on behalf of the people.

Elections were different too. Today, a candidate's name is put formally into a petition signed by ten responsible citizens. He deposits a sum of money as proof of his serious intention to run, and very often sits comfortably in front of a television camera to read a prepared speech. In Howe's day, a man was nominated in person at a large open-air meeting. He then addressed the people from a platform called a hustings, and delivered a bombastic speech interrupted by questions and cat-calls from the crowd. Arguments often developed, which sometimes led to blows, and worse. There is no record of Joe Howe having to use his fists, though he is said to have been expert with them. Perhaps the people in the crowd were more interested in hearing him talk.

"The great cornerstone of the British constitution is responsibility to the people," he boomed at a score of community picnics that summer, soon learning to project his voice over wind, talk, laughter, and the rattle of a late-arriving horse and buggy. It was something new in political speech-making, practical statements instead of oratorical bluster, and it caught the people's attention. "In England the people can breathe the breath of life into their government whenever they please. In this country, the government is like an Egyptian mummy, wrapped up in narrow and antique prejudices, dead and inanimate, yet likely to last forever."

Polling – the counting of votes – was different too. There was no secret ballot. Instead of marking in private a slip of paper with an "X" opposite the name of a candidate as we do today, then depositing it in a sealed box under the eye of scrutineers from both parties, a man cast his vote by shouting out the name of his man, or there was a show of hands. Since the count was made then and there and everyone knew how you voted, you might be threatened with violence by those who heard and disagreed with you. You might even lose your life. "Need we," demanded candidate Howe, "refer to the murders of Pictou and Arichat?" Even the clergy turned out to make sure their parishioners voted according to instructions from the pulpit.

"They tell us Nova Scotia is not ripe for freedom," declared Joe vehemently, "but I say they would sooner see Nova Scotia rotten than ripe!" He told them exactly what he and his running mate meant to do for them if elected. "*One*, reduce the enormous sums spent on the Customs Department; *two*, remove the Bishop from the Council and get rid of the favouritism enjoyed by the Church of England; *three*, establish a sound currency; *four*, gain control of the Casual Revenues, and reduce the high salaries of government officers; *five*, remove the Chief Justice from the Council; and *six*, insist that the Legislative Council open its doors to the public."

He went on to elaborate, and the people settled happily to listen. Political gatherings were all-day outings then, a rare holiday for the farmers and their families, and they enjoyed every minute. So did Joe. He relished the speech-making, delighted in duels of wit with the crowd, loved the hand-shaking and parties afterward. He never had any doubt he would win. After all, since his first journey around Nova Scotia he had without knowing it, been collecting votes.

And so it turned out. At the close of the polls, he and Annand found themselves well and truly elected. In a voice shaken by emotion, Joe addressed the crowd, telling them he had been taught by his father to respect his fellow creatures and do them good. "I hope I have not forgotten and never shall forget the lesson."

"It is clear," said a member of Council sourly, "when such a fellow can be elected, Nova Scotia is no longer fit for gentlemen to live in. But of course he won't last."

"He'll make a fool of himself the first time he stands up in the House."

"Did you hear his speech at the trial?" another asked, meaningfully.

"Yes, but we have our own excellent speakers in the House. Uniacke, Wilkins, Stewart."

The family compact members pricked up their ears. "Alex Stewart? Is he with us now?"

"If he isn't, he soon will be," the reply was tinged with cynicism. "He's a lawyer, and ambitious. He knows who hands out the judgeships."

The other members looked cheered. Perhaps things weren't so bad. After all, speaking in a courtroom was not the same as making oneself heard in Assembly. Parliamentary expertise was needed there.

Joe wasted no time. On the very first day of the first Session of 1837, he made two speeches, one against religious discrimination, and another seconding Doyle's motion that one branch of the legislature sitting in secret to do the public's business was an insult to the people. The resolution passed and was sent up the hall to the legislative chamber while the House went on with other business. A few days later, a reply to the resolution came back. The Legislative Council denied the right of the House to criticize its policies.

Offended and worried by the snub, the Members were uncertain how to act. Elderly John Young, anxious to prevent an open break, moved two resolutions which were nearly apologetic. Joe saw at once that these would lead to the same yielding-under-pressure he had observed in previous assemblies. The time had come, he felt, to grapple with all the problems at once. In place of Young's resolutions, he offered twelve much stronger ones which contained all the points in his and Annand's election platform. If passed in the House, they would go to the Legislative Council for approval, then be forwarded to the colonial office.

The Twelve Resolutions were debated in long, sometimes angry speeches. J.B. Uniacke, leading Tory supporter in the House, scolded Mr. Howe for showing so little respect to the Council as to criticize it. So did his Tory colleague, Lewis Wilkins. Then Alex Stewart made a speech against the Resolutions. This was a surprise. Up to now, Stewart had been a loud advocate of opening the doors and reforming the Council. Last year he had written Joe "I congratulate you on your splendid defence," yet now he set out in a cutting speech to demolish the new Member. Joe put the change down to the *Novascotian*'s criticism of last year's Assembly in which Stewart had supported the motion to increase lawyers' and judges' fees. Stewart, he decided, had gone over to the enemy. He leaned from his chair to whisper to Doyle –

As bees, on flowers alighting, cease their hum,
So, settling on places, Whigs grow dumb.

It looked as though Stewart, like many before him, had recognized the fact that the Assembly had no favours to bestow and no places to give apart from the Speaker's Chair, but the

Council could do much for an ambitious young lawyer. When Stewart finished his speech, Joe rose and gave back as good as he had got.

Others spoke in support, while the "loose fish," those not committed to either side, veered this way and that and, in the final vote, came over to Reform. Then came another message from the legislative chamber saying His Majesty's Council had seen the Twelve Resolutions and objected strongly to the one which charged some of its Members with protecting their own interests at the expense of the public. They hoped the Assembly would not force them to interrupt the public business, which they would have to do, if the offending resolution was not removed.

Dismay seized the House. If they refused to remove the resolution, the Council would make sure the governor dissolved the House and the Revenue Bill would be lost, as it had been lost in the brandy dispute. Heads turned in the direction of the new Member, accusingly.

Outwardly calm, but inwardly shaking, Joe rose to face the Members. He said he was not surprised at the Council's action. "The loss of £40,000 is to be the penalty for telling our King the truth. Can any man now doubt the Council's power or their inclination to protect themselves at this cost to the country?" He sent an encouraging smile around the chamber. "The Council asks us to rescind a particular resolution. I am prepared to give more than they ask"–he paused for a breath–"and rescind them all."

He could feel their amazement and doubt. "I will follow up that motion with another, when the Revenue Bill has safely passed, for the appointment of a committee to draw up an address to the Crown on the state of the colony." Doyle was one of the first to see what was coming and a delighted grin broke over his face. "It is not for me to say, when the committee is appointed, what the address shall contain," Joe went on, "but I presume, having these resolutions before them and knowing how the majority of this Assembly feel about them, they will do their duty."

They all saw it then. The Council could not refuse to do

James B. Uniacke (1800-1885) first premier of Nova Scotia after the
winning of responsible government.

business once the resolution was rescinded. The Revenue Bill
would be saved, but the whole Twelve Resolutions would be
contained in an address to the Throne. It would be clear, too,
that the Council had committed one of the cardinal sins mentioned in the Resolutions, that of holding dissolution over the
heads of the Assembly as a threat if their commands were not
obeyed.

From this moment on, Joe Howe was acknowledged leader
of the Reformers in the House.

The address, drawn up for the most part by Howe, listed
Nova Scotia's complaints and suggested as one remedy the
separation of the Councils; separating them, that is, in the
sense that one man could not sit in both Executive and Legisla-

tive Councils. Vacant seats would thus be provided, to be filled by Reformers as well as additional Tories. The address was carried to the Governor, Sir Colin Campbell, who promised somewhat disapprovingly to transmit it to London.

The other side, waking at last to their danger, hurriedly met to prepare an address of their own, in which they laid great stress on the need for loyalty to the Crown, hinting that the Reformers were about to raise the Stars and Stripes over Province House and spit on the Union Jack. The Governor received this graciously. It was clear which side Sir Colin favoured.

Unobtrusively, however, alterations were begun on the legislative chamber to accommodate members of the public who wished to hear the debates in that chamber. By giving in on what was, to them, a minor point, the councillors hoped to hold fast to others they valued more. They had, of course, taken steps to see that friends in London would make sure their address received preferential treatment at the colonial office.

Meanwhile, in Halifax, there opened a whispering campaign. It was put about that Nova Scotian Reformers were no better than Radicals, like those of Upper and Lower Canada. "It is well known," said the Tory press, "that they are secret followers of Papineau and Mackenzie." Soon Nova Scotia, they suggested, would be stirred to the excited state of Montreal and Kingston. The government officers withdrew their printing from the *Novascotian* and certain merchants stopped advertising in its pages. Many Reformers were dropped from the invitation list at Government House, and were made to feel the weight of the Council's displeasure in other petty ways. Bankers and lawyers were suddenly too busy to see Reformers in their offices, and in Halifax drawing rooms the wives of bankers and judges walked out when a Reformer's wife walked in.

Joe and his group bore all this with what humour and patience they could muster. "Be patient," Joe kept saying, "keep loyal. Say nothing to give them a handle against us and do nothing that will even appear disloyal."

At last one day a message came from Government House: "His Excellency's compliments and would the Honourable

Joseph Howe attend him at eleven on Tuesday morning." The Honourable Joseph Howe would be delighted.

Joe had no way of knowing that the reply to the Reformers' address had arrived, for Sir Colin had revealed this only to his Council. The members had been appalled to learn that the Colonial Secretary, Lord Glenelg, had admitted the Assembly's right to control all provincial revenues, had shut the Chief Justice out of both chambers, and had agreed to the separation of the Councils. When they learned too that the Governor had been instructed to appoint to the vacant seats men who enjoyed the confidence of the great body of the inhabitants, the family compact saw the canyon opening at their feet. They asked Sir Colin Campbell to hold back the dispatch, at least for a time. If things could be straightened out with Lord Glenelg in London, there might be no need in the end to publish it at all. Someone suggested that a good government post ought to be held open for that fellow, Howe, or any other Reformer likely to consider changing sides, and Sir Rupert George hurried off to book a berth on the first vessel bound for England. Meanwhile Sir Colin was to see Mr. Howe and "feel him out."

Joe approached the attractive stone front of Government House that morning, alive with hope and curiosity. As he mounted the stone steps, he reminded himself with amused enjoyment of the countless times he had, during his employment at the Post Office, brought dispatches to this same building, sometimes in the middle of the night and always, of course, to the back door. Now a butler admitted him to the spacious hall with its fine curving stairway, and asked respectfully for his hat and coat. A uniformed aide appeared and showed him through an archway to the Governor's office.

Sir Colin Campbell, a handsome soldierly-looking man, rose and greeted Joe, waving him to a chair on the far side of his desk. Sir Colin did not look a villain, nor was he one. He was neither insensitive nor unkind, but a lifetime in the army, mostly in Spain and India, had persuaded him that a colony was safer in the hands of cultured and wealthy men like Sir Rupert George and the Uniackes than in those of the ignorant natives. He may have noticed that the ordinary Nova Scotian suffered to some extent from the selfishness of the Council, but then no system was perfect. And in what other way could the country be safeguarded against republicanism? Though firmly in the hands of his Council, Sir Colin believed he ruled them. He considered Howe a clever, well-meaning fellow, the one misguided member of a worthy family, and proposed, while feeling out the young man's ambitions, to instruct him in loyalty to the Crown.

After a few minutes of general conversation, His Excellency remarked in a casual way – "Incidentally, Mr. Howe, if, just supposing, the Home government should accede to the Assembly's request for separate Councils, it has occurred to me that I would find it rather difficult to choose a sufficient number of qualified gentlemen in the colony to fill *two* Councils."

His visitor smiled and whipped notepaper from an inside pocket, then begged the use of His Excellency's pen. While Sir Colin Campbell watched, Joe wrote down rather rapidly two lists of names and handed the paper across the desk. "Here, sir, are two lists of eminently qualified gentlemen, men from nearly every county, of all professions, religions, and commercial interests. You will see, too, that I have found places on one or the other for all the present councillors, while at the same time drawing in new blood from the popular party. Huntington, for example, would make an invaluable adviser."

Sir Colin glanced down the list, then went over it again with a puzzled look. "You have omitted your own name." He looked up to meet Joe's quizzical smile.

"Had I included it, your Excellency, my motives would be suspect and my usefulness to the country impaired." If the Governor had indeed considered offering a bribe, he must at this point have dropped the notion, nor did it seem a good time to deliver a lecture on patriotism.

Joe hurried back to his fellow Reformers with the good news. "His Excellency would hardly have talked with me like that if he had not felt the time has arrived to make concessions. Now all we have to do is wait for a reply to our address." He had one private worry at this point. The situation in the Canadas looked bad. If the Reformers on the St. Lawrence declared open revolt, the Tories in Nova Scotia would have a fine whip with which to beat Joe and his friends. Suddenly he had one of his "flashes." ("Knowledge which I never acquired by study," Howe once wrote in his journal, "flashed into my mind as if by inspiration, and a firmness, all unlike my general nature, which is yielding and indifferent enough in small matters, has been vouchsafed to me in my hardest trials.") He remembered the letter from Chapman and his reply in which he had protested Nova Scotia's loyalty with all the eloquence and force at his command. Where was it? He went through the books in which he kept handwritten copies of his important letters, and found the one he wanted. He set it aside, where it would be handy if needed.

The days passed; the autumn came, and the first snow of winter fell. Finally, what he had feared, happened. First, newspapers arrived from the St. Lawrence with headlines reading: "Rioting in Montreal! Scenes of bloodshed!" Then came word that Upper Canada too was in arms.

Joe read the accounts with cold fury. Now the Nova Scotian Reformers would be judged guilty by association.

CHAPTER NINE
1838-1839

*"In one moment British ministers speak the language
of freedom; in the next, the dictatorial style
of a master to his slave."*

Novascotian, January 1839

Joe, of course, published the Chapman letter, which was
widely reprinted in Canadian papers, and true, it did help. It
was the one credit on the side of Reform. Nevertheless, the
triumphant Tories had their whip, and used it unmercifully.
"See what happens," their newspapers cried, "when the people listen to agitators. You have riots and bloody rebellions by
traitors calling themselves Reformers. Do we want this sort of
thing in Nova Scotia? In heaven's name, no!"

The Reformers had to take it and try to smile, but it was a
cheerless time.

They were anxious, too, because they still had not heard
from England in reply to their address. It was decided at last to
send across the ocean a polite note of inquiry. As a result, the
Governor of Nova Scotia shortly received a sharply-worded
order from the colonial office to print the dispatch already in
his possession. Making a virtue of necessity, Sir Colin read it in
his Speech from the Throne on the opening day of the 1838
Session.

It was the Reformers' turn to cheer. The colonial office had
granted nearly all they had asked. There were to be four out-
siders invited into the Executive and it was rumoured that
Huntington, whose name headed Howe's list, had already
been approached to be one of them. The Assembly was invited

94

to accept the Casual Revenues, if they would promise in return to set fair and reasonable salaries.

The Speech also mentioned the death of William IV. The Empire would henceforth be ruled by a Queen, whose name would be Victoria. Finally, the Governor told them that Lord Durham, a prominent English Whig, had just been appointed Governor General of all the British North American colonies and was coming out at once to examine and discover the reasons for the Canadian rebellions.

"Lord Durham," mused Joe as he and his wife left Province House after the opening ceremony, "is known in England as Radical Jack. He was one of the committee of four who drew up the terms of the Reform Bill, so I'd say his appointment is another hopeful sign." He smiled happily as he helped his wife into the sleigh. "First Lord Glenelg gives us all we ask for. Now he sends us a man like Durham."

"It looks, Joseph, as though good may come out of the Rebellions after all," said Susan Ann and he agreed. They bounded homeward over the packed snow to the merry sound of sleighbells.

But almost at once, things began to go wrong.

The Governor announced that a mistake had been made – the Executive was supposed to have had only nine members, not twelve – and when the new list came out, Huntington's name was not included. Joe's list of names had been completely ignored. Seven Anglicans were appointed to the Executive, ten to the Legislative Council and Alexander Stewart was on it as well. In the end, there was not even one Reformer in either Council.

"A mere shuffling of the cards." Joe said bitterly, "The game continues as before."

"One day Britain treats us like free citizens," mourned Doyle, "and the next, like slaves."

Joe showed them a bright side. "We've made gains. We've got different men on the Councils, a few of them from the country. We've forced open the doors of the legislative chamber without physically battering them down. We've got control of the Casual Revenues and can set fair salaries for all officers on the Civil List." He spoke too soon. Though the House passed rather too generous salaries in Joe's opinion, the Legislative Council refused to approve the Assembly's list.

"Very well, we'll send a second address, pointing out that Lord Glenelg's instructions have been disobeyed!"

All that spring there was worrying news from the Canadas. Though the rebellions were put down, there was trouble then on the border, the exiled Mackenzie having been joined by American sympathizers. This created alarm in the British parliament, and the answer to the second address was very different from the first. "Nothing more can be done," announced the Colonial Secretary, "until the rebellions in the Canadas are settled." The Councils, he added, would remain as Sir Colin had designed them, and the Casual Revenues would be retained by the Executive.

Not only was Joe bitterly disappointed by Britain's chopping and changing, he was furious with the Canadas, who to his mind had wiped out all the recent gains made by the Nova Scotians. "There was no justification for a resort to arms," he said angrily.

Someone at that point made the remark that they'd never get anywhere alone. It might be better, after all, to join forces with the Canadians, unite legislatively in some sort of free federation. But Joe, whose fury at that moment was fully directed at the citizenry of Toronto and Montreal, did not take kindly to this suggestion.

"We'd be jumping from the frying pan into the fire," he said sharply. "Nova Scotia is one of the smallest of the provinces. We'd be swamped by the larger ones in any union. We might find ourselves begging at an office in the backwoods of Canada instead of the one in London. No, what we must do is make London hear our side for a change, hear it at last from the lips of a Reformer."

And he told them he would go to England and talk face to face with Lord Glenelg.

Joe Howe sailed early in April, 1838, at his own expense, on the sailing brig *Tyrian* with his friend Tom Haliburton. Three weeks later, when the coast of Cornwall appeared as a deep blue line on the horizon, Joe climbed into a lifeboat for privacy and wrote ecstatic verse in celebration.

> Land of my Fathers, do I then behold
> > Thy noble outline rising from the sea?
> Is this the Isle of which such tales are told
> > Home of the wise, the valiant, and the free?

Not great poetry perhaps, but it came from the heart.

It was the start of a happy and strenuous half-year. Never was there such a tireless tourist as Joe Howe. He missed not a single museum if he could help it, nor a castle, battlefield or stately home. Once in stride, he could walk all day and never tire. "A glance at a place," he told Haliburton, who was taking the whole thing more calmly, having visited Britain before, "is worth a bushel of books."

When the day was over and everyone else asleep, Joe would still be up, writing articles for the *Novascotian*, sending them under a covering letter to Susan Ann with editorial instructions, or filling his diary with notes and impressions. Recalling how, on his way across the Atlantic, the steamer *Sirius* had passed the becalmed *Tyrian*, arriving in England long before her, he thought of Sam Cunard, a Halifax merchant and member of His Majesty's Council, then visiting London. He and Haliburton looked him up at his hotel and suggested he convert his small fleet of schooners to steam as quickly as possible, then apply to carry the transatlantic mails to New York via Halifax. Cunard took the advice and so laid the foundations of a great steamship company. In London, too, Joe helped Haliburton see his book, *The Clockmaker*, through the press. He wrote Susan Ann that thousands of people in the great crowded city were now talking about comical Sam Slick, and he hoped to make something on the book himself to help pay for his trip.

Curiosity took him to all sorts of places. He visited workhouses and hospitals, went down into coal mines and through huge factories where women and small children worked for ten and twelve hours a day for a few shillings. Shocked by much of what he saw, Joe began to wonder how such conditions could be remedied. Why, for example, could not some of England's needy folk be transported to the colonies where poor people had it much easier and where there was opportunity for young people to improve their condition. But would people come? One ill-natured traveller had described Nova Scotia as "a barren, frozen heap of rocks, bogs and mosquitoes." Joe set out to correct this bad impression: "You boast of the fertility and beauty of England," he said, "why there's one valley in Nova Scotia where you can ride for fifty miles under apple blossoms." Even the climate, according to Joe, was perfect. "I rarely wear an overcoat, except when it rains."

"If they beat me at everything else," he told Haliburton, "I ask them how high their tides rise. I've always got them there!" The Fundy tides of Nova Scotia's western shore rise more than forty feet.

He went regularly to the theatre, was enchanted by the actor Kean in *Hamlet*, laughed in music halls until his sides ached, discovered the magic of great music at the opera and concert hall, and ate in restaurants at all hours, usually in the company of interesting new friends. He went to the races at Ascot and saw the Queen, young Victoria, in the Royal Box. "A pretty little girl, not beautiful, but with a sweet expression." He dined with the Irish patriot, Daniel O'Connell, and was given a press pass to the galleries of both Houses of Parliament. He wrote Susan Ann that he had heard there no finer speeches than he heard every day in Province House.

He dined at the Canadian Club and was asked to make a speech. He would love to have gone up in one of the new hot-air balloons, but ten guineas was rather steep. He did get his fortune told at Epsom Downs by the gypsies, for a shilling. Every time he saw a child, he was reminded of his own and wrote his wife that he might be prejudiced, but he had not yet seen a finer lot than his own.

And then he called at the colonial office.

"I sent up my card. They did not name a day to see me," he wrote Susan Ann with pride, "but requested me to come up at once."

Glenelg, an amiable Scot, received him hospitably and they

talked for nearly an hour. "I shall not put anything that passed in a letter, for fear it should fall into other hands," Joe wrote. However, a cryptic note in his diary suggests that their discussion had to do with the Canadian rebellions. This would all be much in both their minds, for Lord Glenelg was being harshly criticized in the House by English statesmen, fearful of border incidents which might lead to war with the United States. His Lordship had been accused of weak handling of the "Canadian Problem." Joe saw now why the Colonial Secretary had made such a curt response to the second address. Glenelg had been trying, too late, to apply a firm hand to the colonies.

No doubt the two men talked as well about Lord Durham's appointment and presence in Quebec at that moment. Glenelg would be able to explain the special powers given this clever, somewhat unconventional statesman, to uncover the reasons for the Rebellions, and why he had taken with him two of England's best-known Colonial Reformers, Charles Buller and Edward Wakefield. This to Joe would look most encouraging. Here were men with sympathy towards Reform, going out to see for themselves what was wrong, and with sufficient powers to do something about it.

He saw Lord Glenelg again before his departure for the continent. Haliburton, meeting him at their lodgings later, thought Joe looked less than cheerful. "How did you get on?"

"Well enough," Joe said absently. "He asked me if there was anything he could do for me at home. Naturally, I said no. The main thing is, the Reformers have now got a friend at court." Haliburton was about to make a sly joke – these two did not always see eye to eye on politics – but then he looked at his friend again. The expressive blue eyes were clouded, the eyebrows seemed to droop. "What's happened to upset you?"

Joe turned on Haliburton a look of wonder and pain. "I dropped by the Club on my way back, to see if there was any mail from home. Cunard was there and asked me over to meet a pair of British industrialists. We chatted for a bit. Then one, out of the blue, said without one least trace of emotion 'England, you know, would be better off without you people. The colonies cost us far too much in defence appropriations. And there's always the danger you'll embroil us in another war with the United States.'"

Haliburton shrugged angrily. "I know. I've met that sort, too. New-rich, self-made men without a thought in their heads but trade and profit. They have no conception of the value of the colonies to the Mother Country – if not at present, then in the future. 'Little Englanders' I've heard them called, and it's an apt description. They'll fight to the death to get a few extra pounds in their cash-boxes, no matter what happens to the Empire."

"Huntington said something to that effect once," Howe said, "but I didn't believe him."

"It's true though. England doesn't value the colonies as she should. Few think as you and I do, that the bonds of Empire ought to be strengthened, not loosened."

This conversation was one Joe remembered often during the journey. It cropped up in all sorts of ways to worry him. Another worry and a more immediate one, however, was Susan Ann, who was expecting a child during his absence. As the day of her confinement drew near, he looked every day for mail, dreading to open a letter with unfamiliar handwriting on the envelope. "I hope and pray," he wrote her, "that God has brought you through handsomely, but the buts and ifs bother me. With you, I feel I can stand against the world. Without you, I would be poor indeed."

At Liverpool, about to take ship for Glasgow, he received a letter at last, but he could tell there must have been an earlier one that he'd missed. This one assumed he knew of the birth.

"I thanked God," he wrote, "that you were both alive, but was puzzled to tell whether it was a boy or a girl till I read 'he thrives well and I never was better,' when you may suppose I was the happiest fellow of the hundred persons on deck, and went up to Scotland with a heart as light as a feather. What does he look like, and what does Josey say of him? How I should love to be in the midst of you all, but must go on till my work, for it has almost ceased to be pleasure, is done. Kiss all the children for me, but particularly the new one. What shall we call him?"

Joe was never to see the baby James. The cause of death is not on record. We do know, however, that in Howe's day there were few effective antiseptics and no antibiotics, so even slight infections could be fatal to an infant.

Joe returned to Halifax to find, as well, that new blows had fallen on his team, and that the fortunes of the Reformers were at their lowest ebb.

CHAPTER TEN
1839

"Let the Majority, not the Minority, govern."

Durham Report,
Novascotian Supplement, 1839

As he had done before, and would do again, Joe put aside the private grief to plunge into work, for it was vital to raise the spirits of his fellow Reformers. After all their fine hopes, Durham had stayed only five months and left in a huff over a disagreement with the British Prime Minister, Lord Melbourne. Joe's colleagues told him that Durham "never went far from Quebec and saw almost nothing of the country. Our delegates travelled up there to tell him about Nova Scotia, but before they'd had time for more than a chat or two, he was off. It's a complete fiasco as far as our cause is concerned."

"We'll manage without him," Joe said firmly.

A real blow was the news that Lord Glenelg too had resigned. They had lost their one friend at the colonial office.

"We'll find another," Joe assured them.

The Reformers themselves were distressed and divided. Some thought both the Executive Council and the Legislative Council should be elected by the people. Some wished to follow the British model, others the American. Joe himself was searching for some system like the British, but without parties. He wanted to eliminate party quarrels and intrigues, and the party discipline which, he thought, was apt to curb initiative and individuality. Huntington, however, declared he would be satisfied with nothing less than complete cabinet government.

102

Herbert Huntington (1799-1851) one of the first Nova Scotia reformers.

The only thing all agreed on was that the people should some-how secure a larger share in governing.

"The time has come," their leader told them, "for us to make a full expression of our grievances, not in an address but through the mouths of properly appointed delegates," and he succeeded in having Huntington and Young sent to England for this purpose. He himself would have enjoyed going, but felt he was needed more at home to keep things steady in the House.

No sooner had the two delegates sailed for England than Sir Colin Campbell sent after them a letter describing the two Reformers as "factious demagogues," quarrelsome agitators in other words, whose grievances were imaginary. He added that he was sending Stewart and Wilkins over to explain the true situation. While the delegates prepared to battle it out in London, the Nova Scotia Assembly settled down to the 1839 Session.

In February, astounding news arrive at Province House. The Americans had invaded New Brunswick! The Maine-New Brunswick boundary had been in dispute for some time, but suddenly the lumbermen on both sides of the border had started shooting at each other. As everyone in the House began exclaiming and asking questions, which no one could answer, Joe had one of his flashes. He jumped to his feet, quelling the angry uproar with a shout – "Mr. Speaker!"

Granted the floor, he moved they adjourn so that a suitable resolution could be framed to help their sister province. There was immediate agreement and a resolution was drawn up with amazing speed. The House voted £100,000 and 8,000 men of the militia to meet the emergency, upon which three rousing cheers were raised for New Brunswick, three more for the Queen, and Mr. Speaker Archibald got so carried away he threw his top hat in the air.

Although at the last moment war was averted and the militiamen were not required, the Assembly's act was not over-looked at Home. And this had been Joe's hope. The affair had served to show Britain in a concrete way that, far from wishing to annex themselves to the United States, the loyal Nova Scotians – of which the majority were those quarrelsome agitators, the Reformers – could be depended upon in time of emergency to stand in the breach for the Mother Country. England, always in dread of war with the Americans, may have felt that in this business Nova Scotia's Reformers had tipped the scales, for the Assembly received a dispatch congratulating the House on its loyalty, and the Reform delegates in London received a fair hearing after all.

Huntington wrote Joe from London. He said Stewart was doing his best to discredit them, raising the usual cry of disloyalty and calling the Reformers a party of rebels, but they had gained certain concessions in spite of him. There would be new free ports opened and post office reforms put into effect. He wrote that he had met and talked with Charles Buller, one of the Colonial Reformers who had helped Lord Durham write his *Report*, and he thought the Nova Scotians had now got another friend at court. "There are those over here, thank God, who seem to understand that self-government is not a prelude to independence. Incidentally, it looks now as though Lord Durham's visit was not the fiasco we thought." Howe was advised to look sharp for the printed version of it, a document which was then being praised in London as one of the greatest British state papers ever written.

Here was encouragement for a change. To have a man like Buller on their side was decidedly hopeful.

When Lord Durham's Report arrived later that Spring, it was like the sun breaking through overcast. It began by suggesting that the two Canadas unite, then went on to speak frankly of the family compacts. "I can conceive of no system so calculated to fill important posts with inefficient persons," Durham wrote. "It is not by weakening but by strengthening the influence of the people that harmony will be secured."

With growing astonishment and delight, Joe read on. "I know not how it is possible to secure that harmony in any other way than *by administering the government on those principles which have been found perfectly efficacious in Great Britain*," in other words, by cabinet government. Ministers must resign when they lost their majority in the House! So there it was at last, thought Joe. Responsible government.

"It surely cannot be the duty of Great Britain to keep a most expensive military possession," Lord Durham wrote, "simply to confer appointments on one, rather than the other, set of persons in the colonies. For this is really the only question at issue." Only five months in the country, thought Joe Howe admiringly, and His Lordship had grasped the whole situation. "I am well aware that many persons will view the system I recommend with considerable alarm, but I cannot conceive of any considerable portion of the people viewing with dissatisfaction a change which would amount simply to this – that *the Crown would henceforth consult the wishes of the people in the choice of its servants*."

It was so right, thought Joe exultantly, so British! Let the majority, not the minority, rule by compelling every governor to select his advisers from among those who enjoyed the confidence of the people and who could prove it by commanding a House majority. It would mean party government, of course, but if Lord Durham thought parties essential, Joe bowed to the inevitable.

How, he wondered, would it be introduced. Further on in the *Report* he found the answer. "The new constitution may be brought into effect by a single dispatch from London," Joe read with satisfaction. As simple as that. No act of parliament, no command from the Queen, was needed – simply a letter or dispatch from the colonial office to Sir Colin. Then it would be up to the Assembly of Nova Scotia. The Reformers would move a "No Confidence" vote in the government and would be certain to win it, and Sir Colin would have no choice but to dismiss the Council. Nova Scotia would then have responsible government!

During the next few months, the Reformers waited confidently for the dispatch. First, Britain's House of Commons would have to consider the Durham Report in detail. Lord Durham would argue eloquently for its adoption, Buller and the other Colonial Reformers would back him up, and then the Members would cast their vote.

"The motion is sure to pass," Joe told his wife.

Alas, when the issue came up in parliament, Lord Durham was too ill to appear and he died some months later. Buller and the others did their best. Buller made the Commons laugh by declaring that, whatever decision Lord John Russell came to, he personally didn't care a pin, because responsible government would inevitably be established by the people themselves. But Lord John, the newest Colonial Secretary, who simply did not believe colonies were capable of ruling themselves, had the last word. He said that he would not under any circumstance consent to the granting of responsible government to the colonies. "If a governor must accept the advice of a colonial cabinet, the connection with England is broken, for how can a governor be responsible to the people and to the Crown at the same time?" Such logic, on which the noble lord prided himself, won the day. The House of Commons turned down Lord Durham's recommendations.

When the news came to Halifax, there was rejoicing in Tory strongholds, and a day of gloom for Howe and his fellow Reformers. Some of them met in the Howe dining-room to express their indignation and talk out their discontent. Joe himself had little to say and, after a while, they left. Then, though it was nearly dark, he got his mare from the shed and went for a long ride in the country to think things over. He came home refreshed and full of energy.

"What are you going to do?" asked Susan Ann, seeing him set out paper and ink.

"Write a letter to Lord John Russell," he answered cheerfully. "I don't think he quite understands the principle of responsible government."

In the next ten days, he wrote not one but four letters to His Lordship and they were "open letters," ones meant to be published as well. They have been described as "the colonial counterpart of Lord Durham's *Report* both in language and logic." Durham wrote from the outside, Howe from personal knowledge and experience. "The people are now tranquil," Durham wrote, "and I believe loyal, determined to abide the decision of the Home government and to defend their property and their country against rebellion and invasion." The voice of the Nova Scotian Reformer was stronger. "All suspicion of disloyalty we cast aside as the product of ignorance or cupidity. We seek for nothing more than British subjects are entitled to, but we will be contented with nothing less."

Joe read over what he'd written. It was unlikely that a lowly assemblyman of one of Britain's smallest colonies could influence the policy of the British colonial office, but he sent the letters just the same.

To understand what effect the letters had on the Colonial Secretary, we must leap the Atlantic and peep into the office of Lord John Russell as he gives last minute instructions to his new Governor General, Charles Poulett Thompson (the future Lord Sydenham), who has just been appointed to succeed Lord Durham as chief administrator of the British American provinces.

"You must not under any circumstances give these frontier politicans the responsible government they ask for," Lord John warned him. The speaker was a small man of deceptively frail appearance (he lived to be nearly ninety), forty-seven at this time and a Whig devoted to parliamentary reform, but not too much reform. Clever, at times short-sighted, he was already famous for his hasty decisions, made without first consulting his party. "And don't encourage party building, Thompson. Parties mean conflict, and the victor always wants sole power. On the other hand," he reflected, "we mustn't push them into another rebellion. In fact, Thompson, seek wherever possible the advice of those who have the community's confidence."

A fine order, thought Thompson. He was to seek the advice of the people out there on the North American continent, but on no account take it. He was to pass on Lord John's orders as unalterable law, but prevent the colonists from rising in arms against colonial office tyranny.

"You need have no trouble if you're tactful," said Russell, reading the other's face correctly. "Defer to their wishes when you can, distract them from idle political talk with plenty of ceremony and civic improvements – but *don't* give them cabinet government."

The future Lord Sydenham was a clever, self-confident man and he said he thought he could manage.

Shortly after Thompson's departure from England, Lord

John received a bulky parcel from Nova Scotia containing four letters from a "frontier politician" by the name of Howe. "Shall I deal with it," the Under-Secretary suggested, but Russell shook his head.

"Let me have them." His Lordship thought, with a sigh, of the endless pages of uninformed argument he must wade through. He began to read.

Soon he lost himself in the clear, colourful incisive prose and was caught up in the generous spirit and intellectual breadth of the writer's mind. Occasionally he laughed aloud at some witticism. Occasionally he frowned at clear-sighted quips at his own department. (It was one of Joe's faults that he was unable to curb his wicked tongue at times, and wit can sometimes cost more than it's worth.) Master Howe, said His Lordship to himself, had better not imagine his scribblings, clever though they be, will win him praise or promotion.

Nevertheless, Lord John Russell had to admit there was nothing small or meanly personal in the writer's views. There were arguments, indeed, which strongly appealed to his logical mind. For example: "The simple and admirable principle of letting the majority govern, you carry into all your corporations, clubs, and public companies and no more suspect that there is danger in it, or that the minority are injured when compelled to submit, than you see injustice in awarding a cup at Epsom Downs to the horse that has won, rather than to the animal which has lost the race."

Another argument struck the Colonial Secretary with even greater force, the part about the governors being controlled by their Councils, since the councillors were appointed "at pleasure" which generally worked out to "life," thus intrenching them securely in office. Lord John looked through the pages until he found the passage and read it again: "It is a mockery to say that the governor himself is responsible, for he must carry on the government by and with the few officials he finds in possession when he arrives. He may flutter and struggle in the net, as some well-meaning governors have done, but he must at last resign himself to his fate and, like a snared bird, be content with the narrow limits assigned him by his keepers." This, thought Russell with alarm, must not happen to Governor General Thompson.

He sent for his secretary and dictated, rather hastily, a dispatch stating that councillors must not in future hold their places for life. "*Not only will such officers be called upon to retire from the public service as any sufficient motives of public policy may suggest the expediency of that measure, but a change in the person of the governor will be considered as sufficient reason.*" Lord John's mind must have been wandering at that moment, for his words could be interpreted in various ways – as the right of a governor to dismiss councillors who didn't suit him, as the right to dismiss a whole Council if the people disapproved of it, or as the right – if he happened to be newly-appointed – to dismiss a government without cause. At the moment Russell was only concerned to keep Thompson from becoming a snared bird. He added the date to his dispatch – October 16, 1839.

Having arrived at Quebec, Lord Sydenham, as we may now call him, formally accepted the government of all British North America and in his first speech was careful not to mention the objectionable words "responsible government."

"I have received the Queen's commands," he said, "*to govern in accordance with the well understood wishes and interests of the people.*" The wording was not that of Lord John's last instruction "to seek the advice of those in the confidence of the community," and could only lead to further misunderstanding.

When a copy of the speech arrived at Halifax, the Reformers were unhappy because there was no mention of responsible government. Without that, the Queen's command was of course impossible to follow. "How is a governor to know what the well-understood wishes of the people *are*?" Joe demanded, "without a vote of the people's representatives?"

Huntington nodded morosely. "And with an appointed Council holding office for life, it would do no good if he did know."

When, therefore, Lord John Russell's dispatch of October

16th appeared in the *Gazette* soon after, to the effect that councillors could no longer hold office for life, Joe read it at first with astonishment. *"Not only will such officers be called upon to retire from the public service as any sufficient motives of public policy may suggest the expediency of that measure, but a change in the person of the governor will be considered as sufficient reason."* He saw the ambiguities of the wording, but his mind took a leap over them. He carried the paper to Huntington and gave it to him to read, wondering if his own eyes had deceived him. The Yarmouth Member read at first with a puzzled frown, then with dawning hope. "What exactly could this mean to us?" he asked slowly.

"It means" – said Joe in a low, excited voice – "it means that men holding office in government – Wallace, Jeffrey, Halliburton, the lot of them – must resign when the governor says public policy demands it!"

"And how does the governor know when public policy demands it?" Huntington asked, his eyes beginning to gleam.

"By a vote of the House of Assembly of course."

"And that means?"

"The bringing in of responsible government! What stronger motive of public policy could there be than a vote of the people's representatives that the government has lost the people's confidence?"

"Wait a minute," the other said with belated caution. "There's nothing here about responsible government."

"But," said Joe in triumph, "the Governor General has told us his instruction from the Queen is to govern *according to the well understood wishes of the people.* Put his speech and this dispatch together, and we've got all we need."

Huntington seldom smiled, but he was smiling now. "By Jove, Howe, those letters of yours seem to have borne good fruit!"

The House opened on February 3, 1840, and Joe was the first to rise and move four resolutions which for the first time in Nova Scotia constituted a motion of "No Confidence" in the government. It was an historic moment. In the debate which followed, Reform and Tory members defended their

111

opposing views. Supporters of the family compact took the stand that the dispatch of October 16 was merely a way of strengthening the governor's power, which was of course, as we know, what Lord John intended. Uniacke insisted that it did not give Nova Scotia a new constitution, as the Reformers claimed. The Reformers pointed to New Brunswick, where the governor of that province had accepted it as such and had already put it into effect.

It was no battle of Bunker Hill, no Canadian Rebellion. There were no bullets, no blood. It was a momentous conflict all the same, and one which would influence the progress of Reform in all the colonies of the Empire. It was one, it must also be remembered, in which there would be stern penalties for the losers. If the supporters of Torydom won out, the Reformers would feel their power for years to come. If Reform prevailed, the Tories would lose their fat salaries and privileges, perhaps forever.

So the teams struggled back and forth in the legislative arena, using every art of persuasion and eloquence they knew. A rush was stopped here, a shot deflected there, but the big advance came near the end of the debate when James B. Uniacke rose and admitted he was convinced that, after all, the dispatch did give a new and improved constitution to Nova Scotia. The province must claim her right to participate in responsible government without delay. He would support the motion of "No Confidence" and if it passed, would set an example by resigning his own office. This was a hard blow to the Council and caused many "loose fish" to be won over to Reform. By the end of the third day – February 5, 1840 – when a final vote was taken, it was thirty to twelve in favour of the "No Confidence" motion.

Triumphantly, the House asked Sir Colin Campbell to demand the resignation of the Council.

But this Sir Colin refused to do.

CHAPTER ELEVEN
1840

"I feel that I am bound to hazard my life."

> Letter to the People of Nova Scotia,
> March 1840

'I have every reason," said Sir Colin austerely, "to be satisfied with the advice and assistance which the present Executive Council have at all times afforded me." He said bluntly that he did not believe the colonial office had granted responsible government. He had instructions from Lord John Russell based on an earlier dispatch which stated that he could not dismiss the whole Council, only individual members. The Reformers argued that the later dispatch cancelled the earlier one. Sir Colin, offered several chances to reconsider, refused to dismiss his Council for any reason whatsoever.

The next move to Joe was obvious. "A change in the person of the governor," he reminded his fellow Reformers, "will be considered *sufficient reason for the Executive Council to retire.* We must ask the Queen to recall Sir Colin Campbell."

At once there was an uproar. It was one thing to attack the Tories, the Executive, and its supporters in the House, but quite another to roughly handle a representative of the Queen, for in that day the dignity of a governor was nearly as great as the sovereign's. Sir Colin, moreover, was generally well liked and respected. Recall would reflect on his ability and tact.

Joe pointed out that a choice had to be made all the same, between devotion to the Crown and loyalty to the people. Which was it to be – the people or the governor? Respect for

113

the Crown or fair play for Nova Scotia? He knew it was a hard decision, and he confessed that he himself felt like a soldier called out on a firing party to shoot a man who had been forced by bad advisers into crime.

Huntington made the motion for the governor's recall and the question was thrashed out on the floor of the House until it passed by two-thirds of the vote. Then, oddly enough, members of Council who had never before thought it necessary to consult the people, suddenly moved the battle into the streets and countryside, holding meetings and making heated speeches in defence of Sir Colin. The Tory papers, too, professed to be highly indignant at what the Reformers were doing to the poor governor. "We *said* they were no better than rebels!"

"It is wrong," declared Solicitor General James W. Johnston, "to send home in his old age, disgraced, a man who has served so bravely as a soldier." This was the same lawyer, Johnston, to whom Joe had applied when he was seeking help for Andrew Brown.

"Remember Wellington," Joe advised the Tory lawyer, "who, though the greatest captain of the age, was driven out of government by the people of England because they did not like his politics." This was the first clash between the two leaders.

The Tories, alive at last to their danger, looked at Joe Howe with hatred and disbelief. How had this vulgar self-educated printer's boy managed to place them in such a galling position? The fellow had had the indecency to write letters to the Colonial Secretary in which they, the leading members of Halifax society, had been accused of greed and self-interest. The letters had been published, too, for all to read.

Certain relatives of Joe's deserted him at this time. Jane, of course, and his mother, never wavered, and there was a nephew, William Howe, son of Joe's half-brother David, who openly declared his allegiance to Uncle Joe. The rest were fearful of being judged and punished for his sins, like John who, though fond of his young brother, was beholden to Tory masters for his jobs of Postmaster and Queen's Printer. For the first time Joe felt thankful his father was no longer alive, to be saddened by the division of the family.

114

Old friends, too, turned against him. Tom Haliburton, whose judgeship had put out the brief fire of Reform in him, attacked and made fun of "the Reformer" in his latest Sam Slick book. Though Joe told the resentful Susan Ann not to mind, "It's just politics," he was deeply hurt. "They scorn me at their feasts," he once burst out to Jane, "and insult me at their funerals."

Younger members of Tory families drank deep and swore to horsewhip "that devil, Howe" or duck him in the horse pond. They even talked of challenging him to a duel, but in sober moments remembered his skill with a pistol. So, for a while, no one could be found to sacrifice himself. One day, however in a passion over a piece in the *Novascotian* criticizing his father, young Dr. William Almon called Howe out, but friends on both sides got together and stopped this meeting. Then came a challenge from John Halliburton, son of the Chief Justice, who objected to remarks in the *Novascotian* about *his* father. He demanded an apology or a meeting and Joe agreed to meet him. He confided only in Huntington, who was horrified.

"Have nothing to do with it," he cried, "it's illegal, in the first place. And either way, they win. If you kill their man, you'll be up for murder. If he kills you ..." Huntington left it there. "Apologize, Howe. Do whatever is necessary to avoid a meeting."

"I'll only be called out later by someone else. And if I keep avoiding it, I'll be called a coward."

"What does that matter? It's moral courage you need in this game. Brute courage is nothing."

"I know that," Joe said soberly. "I'd sooner stand a shot any day than introduce the Twelve Resolutions again, or have to defend myself a second time on a libel charge. I hate and detest the custom of duelling as much as you do Huntington. It's snobbish, and it defies God's law against shedding blood. But I don't see how I can avoid it, and still be of any use to the country. If I draw back, it will weaken my position as a public man. That's probably what they're after. I've never made a secret of how I feel about these meetings."

115

Huntington gave him a worried glance. "And if you kill Halliburton?"

"No danger," Joe said cheerfully, "I'll fire over his head."

"But then–" Huntington paused. "We can't afford to lose you," he said bluntly.

Joe asked if Huntington would be his second.

"Why me?"

"Because I know I can depend on you."

Huntington gave up the struggle. "Very well," he said, "but I warn you I'll do all I can to get the business settled off the field." He tried, but was unsuccessful.

The night before the meeting, Joe wrote several letters, to be delivered if he should be killed. One was to Susan Ann. "I cannot trust myself to write what I feel," he said. "You had my boyish heart, and have shared my love and entire confidence up to this hour. Heaven and ourselves only know the pure pleasures of the past. The future for you and my dear babes might well unman me and would, did I not feel that without a protector you could better face the world than with one whose courage was suspected, and who was liable to continual insult which he could not resent. God in his infinite mercy bless you. There shall be no blood on my hand. Yours till death."

In his letter to the people of Nova Scotia, he simply explained that any doubt of his courage would have a bad effect on the fight he was waging for their rights, and so he had thought it necessary to hazard his life in this way.

He rose early that chill March morning without waking Susan Ann, dressed quickly and spent a few moments in the nursery. Then he let himself quietly out of the house. Huntington was waiting down the road with horse and wagon.

"You'll not change your mind." It was not a question, but a statement, and Joe only answered with a shake of the head. They clopped through the silent streets, Joe surprised to find that he felt a curious lack of anxiety, only an impatience to get the thing over and done with. The matter had been settled. Nothing to do now but go through the motions, stand up and make a target of himself.

They turned into the Tower Road very close to the cottage

116

where Joe had spent his childhood, and the happy recollection of those sunlit days was followed by a flood of desolation. He didn't want this to be all there was ...

Then the woods closed around them, and in a moment the wagon rattled to a stop beside Martello Tower. There at the edge of the clearing stood the silent group.

Putting all weakening thoughts aside, Joe jumped down and strode to meet the enemy.

Young Halliburton, very white around the mouth, was holding himself stiffly. On horseback in the background sat an army doctor, pressed into service under a vow of secrecy. A few years earlier, the opponent of a Uniacke had died for lack of prompt medical aid.

Huntington went aside with the other second and they spoke together for a moment, then came to the two principals and made one last effort to settle the quarrel. Joe looked intently at Halliburton, but when the young man shook his head, he shrugged, thanked the two seconds for their help and chose a weapon at random from the gun-box. Against the warm flesh of his hand, the butt felt icy. The two seconds measured the ground, then moved the duellists into position. Joe's heart began to thump unevenly as he awaited the signal –

The square of white linen dropped.

Firing arm still at his side, Joe stood like a rock. The sound of the shot made him jump, but he felt nothing. He knew then with a great surge of thankfulness he had not been hit. He paused, slowly raised his arm and took careful aim. Then, savouring the moment to the full, he said with the ghost of a laugh, "Let the creature live!" and shot into the air.

No breakfast had ever tasted so good as the one he ate that morning. Susan Ann must have wondered why her husband was so unusually talkative, so full of mirth and affection towards the children. When the little ones had finished and left the table, Joe told his wife what had happened. Naturally she was horrified. He hastened to reassure her.

"Think of it this way, Susie. Now and in the future I can laugh at anyone who calls me out."

And laugh he did when, a short time after, Sir Rupert

George sent a note through John Spry Morris demanding satisfaction for an editorial calling him "a red tape man." Joe reached happily for pen and paper and wrote Morris as follows: "Having never had any personal quarrel with Sir Rupert George, I should certainly not fire at him if I went out, and I have no great fancy for being shot at whenever public officers, whose abilities I may happen to contrast with their emoluments, think fit to consider political argument and general illustrations insolent and offensive."

The words of the reply soon got out and were repeated with relish all over town.

Meanwhile the address of censure, asking for Sir Colin's recall had travelled across the sea to Lord John Russell who, when he read it, was flabbergasted. "They want me to recall the Governor! What impudence!" Twenty-five Members had voted in favour of the address, a majority, but that made no difference. He had *not* granted the colonists *responsible government*! Lord John was so upset he dictated two dispatches on the same day, one saying the address was most irregular and he wouldn't dream of submitting it to Her Majesty, the other saying "the Queen has remarked with pain the demand for Sir Colin's recall."

That afternoon, however, when he was cooler, he picked up the copy of his ill-fated dispatch to Sydenham and read it, seeing how it did indeed lend itself to misunderstanding. He glanced too over several of Sir Colin's recent dispatches, which stated that the Reformers were simply a few rebels who wished to force Nova Scotia into separating from the Empire. More than a few, thought Lord John, if the two-thirds vote on the "No Confidence" motion was any guide. The Under-Secretary agreed that most of Sir Colin's dispatches indicated strong prejudice, and Russell recalled that when the Governor had taken Huntington into the Council, Reformer Huntington was part of a majority of thirty-to-one, yet was outnumbered by Tories in the Council eleven-to-one.

"Some changes must be made," Russell acknowledged, but then his expression hardened. "Nevertheless Sir Colin was

118

right about the meaning of the dispatch and the Reformers wrong." He wavered. "But I can't say that. If I do, I admit it's our intention to employ men in the colonies who do *not* enjoy the confidence of the people, which could lead to another War of Independence! If you ask me, that chap Howe knew very well what my real intention was. He's simply using my dispatch to force responsible government on me." Angrily the Colonial Secretary rubbed his nose. The Under-Secretary, who had served under previous office holders, had a suggestion: "Why not leave it to the Governor General. He knows your wishes. I understand one can leave Quebec in that new steamer of Mr. Cunard's and be at Halifax in three days or less."

Johnny Russell, as he was known in government circles, breathed a sigh of relief. "Take a very private and confidential letter to Lord Sydenham."

The duel had taken place in March of 1840. On July 9 of the same year, the *Unicorn* arrived at Halifax with Lord Sydenham aboard. The cheers of the crowd at the dock were perhaps as much for the 300 horsepower engines of the Cunard ship as for the Governor General. Men hung about the wharf long after he'd driven away to Government House.

Sydenham came braced for the work ahead, confident he could snatch victory from the threat of defeat. He was a man who relied on expedience – what would work, that is, rather than what was ethical. When expedience rather than principle is the rule, double-dealing may be expected. He had decided that coalitions would best answer Russell's complicated require- ments. If a few Reformers were put into each colonial Execu- tive, the Tory Compact would be broken up and there would be a mixed government of Tories and Reformers, which would evade a complete change of councillors and so keep respon- sible government at bay. He would then make it a rule that any office holder must first get himself elected to the Assembly. There, the office holder would act, not only as the people's representative, but also as the governor's man. Knowing he could be dismissed from office if he did not do as the governor wished, the Member would be obedient and sway those in the

Assembly who were not office holders to the same obedience. The Assembly would control the Council in theory – the governor would control it in fact.

He needn't explain all this in so many words. He would be tactful and persuasive and tell each side what they wished to hear, making them believe coalition government would serve each best.

Joe, as leader of his party, was the first to be invited to the viceregal presence. He went to Government House with happy expectancy, certain London was ready at last to bow to the will of the people. He was prepared to like Sydenham. He had heard of him as a man who had reached high place from quite lowly beginnings, through sheer merit and energy. Here was someone he could admire and emulate.

Meeting him, Joe saw a short, rather portly man of under forty, with a pleasant but penetrating eye. Within the hour, Joe Howe fell into such a state of hero worship he was a long time recovering from it, if indeed he ever did, for three years later, when his fourth son was born, he named the boy Sydenham Howe.

Seated side by side on a velvet sofa in the Government House sitting room, Joe was encouraged to read aloud from his four open letters to Lord John Russell, in order to show that there was no treason in his efforts to secure responsible government. Sydenham stopped him now and then to ask a question, and congratulated him at the end on his careful and selfless presentation. By then, having sized up his man, His Excellency judged the time right to confess that the arrangement he was instructed to make might not entirely please the Reformers. "It is agreed, of course, that the old system, absurd and unfair as it always has been, is doomed. Sir Colin will be recalled and a new system inaugurated." So far, so good, thought Joe.

"A strong British liberal," Sydenham said, "will replace Sir Colin, will dismiss the present Council and form a new one, probably smaller, but made up of men from both parties." Come now, Joe asked himself, what was wrong with that? He had nothing against combining men of differing views in government, preferring it in fact to a single-party-in-government system. "I will be frank with you, Mr. Howe." The Governor General lowered his voice to a confidential tone. "Elections take place soon in a united Canada. There will be difficulties in reconciling French and English, and in fact the whole situation may be troublesome. If you, in Nova Scotia, would set an example of co-operation, of moderation and loyalty, it would help my task immeasurably." If he had judged his man correctly, Howe would rise to the bait.

"So far, Your Excellency," Joe said with pride, "our fight has been constitutional and bloodless. I intend it shall be so to the end." This was what Sydenham had hoped to hear.

"Lord John's idea," he continued, "is to form a strong mixed Executive Council which will remain in power only while it has the support of the majority of the House." He saw Howe nod approval. "If outvoted by that majority, the governor must dismiss it and choose a new Council." But, practically speaking, thought Joe, that was responsible government.

"This new Executive," Sydenham continued, "will be composed of nine rather than twelve members. The gentlemen on the Council who at present have no seat in either the Legislative Council or the Assembly, will be asked to retire. You and two other Reformers will take their places."

Himself and two others. Six to three in other words. Joe sank back against the velvet cushions, disappointed. He had certainly not expected a coalition in which Reformers would be in a minority.

"I can promise, of course," said the Governor General quickly, reading his expression, "that others of your party will be called in as vacancies occur, until the Cabinet consists altogether of talented men from both sides." That had a better sound, especially the word "Cabinet."

"Responsible government by degrees," he said slowly, remembering Jane's plant metaphor.

"Quite," said Lord Sydenham with a smile.

Learning by experience, thought Howe, working things out by trial and error, that was the way. Ever since the Canadian rebellions Joe had feared untried theory. To him, therefore, a mixed government – temporarily of course – sounded fine. Of course the others might not agree. Some of them would be certain he favoured it because he himself would be a member of the Executive Council. "I think it would please my party better if you were to leave me out," he said. He wanted badly to take an active part in the coalition, but now was the time for thinking what might or might not work. Sydenham shook his head.

"We must be sure the Assembly will support the new system, Mr. Howe, which they are far more apt to do with you in the Executive. Besides, I shall expect you to guide your Tory colleagues to an understanding of the new principles." New system, thought Joe with sudden amusement, new principles; how careful His Lordship was to avoid the words "responsible government." He smiled too at the thought of Wilkins, Johnston and Stewart being instructed by the upstart, Howe, in the principles of the new system. "Will the Tories agree to a mixed government?" he asked Sydenham.

"They have no choice," His Excellency said. "You will also be required to help and advise the new Governor, Lord Falkland."

So Lord Falkland was to replace Sir Colin Campbell. Joe had heard of him. Married to the illegitimate daughter of King William Fourth, he had been a Whig Member of Parliament. Joe would not have been human if he had not relished the thought of becoming special adviser to a governor and a lord. More to the point was the fact that Falkland was a liberal sympathetic to parliamentary reform.

Just the same, Joe returned to the one aspect of the coalition which disturbed him, the ratio of Tories to Reformers – or "Liberals," as most of his party now called themselves, the Tories having, around the same time, become "Conservatives." "With our majority in the House, surely we should have it also, sir, in the Executive?"

"Is the time right for that, Mr. Howe?" Sydenham inquired gravely. "Lord John thinks not. It might lead to the Conservatives taking a stand for party government, or possibly your own people, with a taste of power, might hasten things with an armed uprising." He had touched a nerve there, had said the one thing calculated to win Joe over. Shrewdly reading Joe's reaction, the Governor General pressed his advantage. "The old Council of Twelve will be broken up, its remaining members 'reformed' by association with you and your colleagues. All patronage will be out of their hands." That was important, thought Joe, very important. Sydenham was waiting for his answer.

"Is this what Britain wants?" he asked directly. The other nodded firmly. "Then, if it is clearly understood the Executive will resign on a vote of want of confidence, and if Lord Falkland will agree to take in additional members of my party at the first opportunity" – he paused, took a deep breath – "I shall do my best to persuade my friends to accept the arrangement."

"Thank you, Mr. Howe." Seeing relief in Sydenham's eyes, Joe added warmly: "I will see that Nova Scotia does everything possible to make your job in Canada successful." And, in a sudden rush of generous enthusiasm, he offered to serve in the new Council two years without office or reward, so that no one could say he was doing it for personal gain.

Was it kind then, or fair, of the cynical Lord Sydenham to write the Colonial Secretary that he had seen and talked with Howe, a man driven by "petty and personal ambition," and had converted him to coalition? "I have read people, parties, Assembly and all, a good lecture," he added, "and have placed a decided negative on the demand for what is called responsible government," which was scarcely the truth.

He steamed back to Quebec, satisfied he had made a success of his mission, and so he had. He had set back the cause of responsible government eight years.

CHAPTER TWELVE
1840-1843

"Our duty is to give Lord Falkland a generous and manly support."

Speech, Reform Dinner, 1840

Joe knew it would not be easy to win the Assembly's support to the new system, knew too that Huntington would be the hardest to convince. If he could win over that man of rigid opinions, he would be half way to success.

"Believe me, old man," he said persuasively, "the evolutionary way is best."

Huntington's eyes remained cold. "Your enemies will say you have sold your principles for office."

"What my enemies say won't bother me." But the charge hurt.

"And your friends," Huntington grated on, "will take sides, thus splitting our party down the middle just as our membership is growing strong."

"Not when the new system is explained to them, Huntington. In time, and Lord Sydenham has promised this solemnly, we will have a proper Cabinet made up mostly of Liberals. Meanwhile we have responsible government in all but name."

"Never! Not without one party in power, the other in opposition." The voice was hard with conviction. "A mixed administration can never act according to the people's wishes, because they have no way of finding out what those wishes are. That is what parties are for. Each stands for a different principle, a different plan of action, which is explained to the people before an election. Then the people, by choosing one party instead of the other, tell us what they want."

"Very true, Huntington, but it's not time for that yet. The people must be educated to the new principles gradually. What is needed now is a strong government in which privilege has no place, one based on the confidence of the country and peacefully sustained by a majority of the representatives."

"We have a majority now on almost every issue," Huntington said, exasperated. "Yet only two Liberals are to be taken into the Executive. We aren't moving ahead, we're moving sideways. Instead of an all-powerful family compact, we'll have an all-powerful governor."

"We'll have a governor obliged to ask for the Executive's resignation," Joe contradicted, "when it loses the confidence of the people. You'll be part of that Executive, old man, able to give the governor good advice" – he paused, seeing Huntington's sharp gesture of negation. "I was counting on you!"

"No." Implacability was written plain on the rugged face. "I'll stick by the old cause. It's party government or nothing."

But Joe too was firm. He would stand by his promise to Sydenham, firm in his conviction that full responsible government must be won by degrees, no matter if half the party disapproved, which it did. He had to work very hard to get a majority in the House to back the new system, pleading with all the energy and eloquence at his command: "Let us make Nova Scotia, by her loyalty, intelligence and spirit, a normal school for the other provinces."

He got his majority, but Huntington and a few others promised they would seize the first chance to bring down the mixed government. Cheerfully, Joe admitted their right to try.

All went well at the start. Lord Falkland, a handsome, haughty young man with a pretty wife, arrived in 1840 and invited Howe, S.G.W. Archibald and James McNab into the new Executive Council. Joe's brother-in-law, James McNab, was the second and only other Liberal, for Archibald was neutral, voting on issues rather than by party. When, shortly after, he was promoted to Master of the Rolls, Lord Falkland brought in another Liberal, William Young. When Young retired to accept a judgeship, the vacancy in the Executive was not filled at once. The majority of the Executive, therefore, consisted of Conservatives. They were James W. Johnston, Sir Rupert George, Alexander Stewart, two other members of the old compact, Councillors Dodd and DeWolf, and James B. Uniacke. Uniacke, though he had voted with the Reformers on the "No Confidence" motion, was still a Tory, though a somewhat unhappy one. He was being treated coldly by many of his old colleagues and called traitor behind his back.

Four other Tories, Jeffrey, Cogswell, Collins and Tobin, had received notice to quit. Seeing their former seats occupied by "those two agitators," they burned with humiliated pride, and from the start combined with Tory relatives and friends to wage a malicious underground war against governor and coalition.

At first meeting, Lord Falkland and Joseph Howe got on well. The two young men found themselves in agreement on many subjects, Lord Falkland promising to bring more Liberals into the Council at the earliest opportunity. "Whatever Lord John Russell may say," he confided to his chief minister, "I believe full responsible government, party government that is, must come, and soon." Delighted to find the young nobleman so well disposed toward reform and so friendly toward himself, the *Novascotian*'s editor praised His Lordship extravagantly: "Now is the winter of our discontent made glorious summer by the sun of Falkland!" If Joe Howe had anything to do with it, the Governor's administration would be the most popular one in Nova Scotia's history.

In November, Joe won his seat in the House without difficulty and was also elected by his colleagues in the Assembly to the Speakership, an honour for one so young and one which provided him with a much needed salary. The Liberals soon demonstrated their regular majority in the House and Joe might have been justified in claiming for his party at least half the seats in the Executive, but, mindful of his promise to Sydenham, he did not do so.

The year 1841 was one of the busiest of his life. As "Mr.

Editor" he kept in regular communication with the people; as Councillor Howe, he did his tactful best to educate the other councillors in the principles of responsible government; as Mr. Speaker Howe, he came down regularly from his high place to arbitrate and calm the troubled waters of the Assembly; and as Chief Adviser Howe, he led a proud, wilful young man in the way Lord Sydenham wanted him to go. There were times when he felt like a juggler – deft, exhilarated, but rather too busy.

In June he and Susan Ann travelled to Kingston to take part in the ceremonies attending the union of the Canadas and to be gratified by the sincere congratulations of Lord Sydenham who, having by then had hard experience of his own in running coalitions, knew what Howe must have been going through in Nova Scotia. "You have done marvellously, my dear fellow," he said with warmth, "Be sure to call on me, however, if you should ever need help." He introduced the Howes to all the leading men in Canadian business and politics and took pains to see they were well entertained in Kingston society.

Joe had just taken up his burdens in Nova Scotia again when, in September of that same year, came word that Sydenham was dead. Beyond the sorrow and shock, Joe felt also a kind of loneliness. He was on his own now. Of course, there was McNab, and he was fortunate to have at his shoulder so loyal and dependable a colleague, but the main burden would fall on Joe himself. In December, therefore, he determined to make politics his full time career, and sold the *Novascotian*. It was like parting with a child, but he knew it had to be done. He sold it to a man named Nugent who had to give it up after a year or two, when ownership was transferred to Will Annand.

Early in 1842, Councillor Howe had to meet the first real threat to the coalition. The attitude of the Conservative councillors to their Liberal brothers in the Executive had up till then been pleasant and courteous – on the surface, at least – but that spring there was a subtle change. News had come from England that the Whigs were out of office and Tory hopes suddenly revived. No longer, they told themselves, could Lord Falkland show favouritism to the Liberals. Now his chief at the colonial office was a Conservative and, since Lord Stanley was known to be even more strongly opposed to party government than Lord John Russell, the Tories in the Council let it be known that they too were against it. It was the old family compact tactic, to gain the support of governor and colonial office.

Alex Stewart made a speech in the Legislative Council saying there was no such thing as responsible government in Nova Scotia, it was "responsible nonsense." If it were in effect, he said, it would be independence. Johnston said much the same thing, but in more cautious language. Here were two ministers, working with Howe and McNab to run the country on the new system, publicly denying the principles of that new system. As these principles were the ones Howe had told the Assembly the government would follow, and since the Assembly would never have supported the government so loyally for over a year otherwise, he was naturally incensed.

"If any man says there has been no change," he said, directing wrathful eyes around the silent legislative chamber, "the person speaking does not state what is a fact." And he threatened to retire and allow the Assembly to try a vote of "No Confidence" if the Members did not retract. Alarmed for their offices, the Tory councillors arranged for Dodd to make a blanket denial of what had been stated.

The danger passed for the moment, but confidence in the new government had been shaken.

Lord Falkland privately blamed ex-Councillors Collins, Cogswell, Tobin and Jeffrey for much of the trouble. They were men of wealth, with influence over a horde of Tory job-holders, and they had been able to mount a well-organized war of attrition through the press and also by means of a whispering campaign in Halifax society. "With their vile articles," Lord Falkland exclaimed, "their petty quarrels and their mistaken ideas of their own importance, they make my position in society intolerable!" Again Howe relieved some of the strain by writing anonymous letters in the *Novascotian*, in which he strongly defended His Lordship and the government. Privately, he warned Lord Falkland to be careful of what he said before the Council, for most of its members were friends of the Collins crowd and had been for many years.

Early in the second Session, the Honourable Joseph Howe suggested a program of aid to the Micmac Indians of the province. When reminded of the lack of funds for such a purpose, he said he was sure that whoever was appointed commissioner would serve without fee, if his mere expenses were paid. Apparently no other member of the Executive felt as he did about the native people, for that autumn Indian Commissioner Howe made his first report to the Assembly: "In a drizzling rain, we followed blind paths through the forest and finally arrived on the margin of Lake Kejemakoojik about an hour before dark, completely drenched. We got a boat there, and after rowing a mile or so, arrived in front of Jeremy's clearing. The Indian was away, but his wife was home and a message dispatched to a neighbouring camp soon brought half a dozen swarthy fellows with a carload of moosemeat. Fried in caribou fat and with good potatoes and a cup of tea, we felt much better and soon got our wet clothing dried in front of the fire. In the morning we paddled around much of the lake to look at the wild meadows skirting its shores and to see what progress had already been made in the way of agriculture."

There is no sound of complaint here, rather one of zest, as if he found the roads and swamps a relief after the rigours of the coalition. For by that time, troubles were piling up one upon another. They began as the Howes were visited by a private tragedy. Joe's brothers, John and William Howe, had died within a few days of each other, William by his own hand, and at the same time word came from Jane that her son had been lost at sea. The warm sympathy of Governor Falkland and his wife consoled Joe to some small degree, and his regard for Lord Falkland soared higher than ever.

This was a time also when Joe's influence with the party was less than it had ever been before, and when much of his popularity with the people had been lost because he had, as some saw it, joined forces with the enemy. Huntington nearly won a

"No Confidence" vote that year, and several government bills were defeated.

As a partial solution, Howe asked Lord Falkland to bring another Liberal into the Executive to fill the vacancy left by Young. Once again Huntington was approached, but once again refused to sit on a coalition Executive. The office of Provincial Secretary being vacant at that time, Howe applied for it on the ground that Lord Falkland could best use him there to strengthen the government. Whether his asking offended the Governor or for some other reason, Lord Falkland made him Minister of Excise and Impost instead, softening the blow with a warm compliment: "I am quite sure that my having it in my power to name you will not give you half the pleasure it has given me."

It was a relief to the Howes at any rate, to have a regular income once more, for the year 1842 also marked the start of their financial troubles. Because of his promise to work for the new system without pay for two years, Joe had so far had only his Speaker's honorarium and a part of the money from the sale of the newspaper. According to Mrs. Howe, they never did receive the full purchase price. With this limited income, Joe for the best part of two years had to provide for a large family and meet the expenses expected of him as a public man. Necessity drove him at last to hire a lawyer named Peter Lynch to collect money owed to him, and Lynch records what happened: "He then regularly wrote me day by day, telling me not to proceed against such a one because he was honest but poor, such another as he was too good a fellow to press, such another as he had a large family." "Eventually," Lynch writes, "Mr. Howe asked for his books back, saying, 'Oh don't bother any more about them. I know the fellows are fooling me, but I can't press them. If they pay me, well and good, and if not, I can do without it.'"

He had no qualms, though, about pressing the proprietors of the *Baptist Messenger* who, he claimed, had for some time owed the *Novascotian* a large printing bill. When he publicly accused them of failing to honour their obligations, Johnston stepped into the quarrel on the side of the *Messenger* and through its pages berated his colleague on the Council for making false charges. If it had not been already sufficiently plain to the country that the Members of the unpopular coalition were at odds, it was then, and Howe was highly annoyed with Johnston. Shortly after their acrimonious exchange, Howe was told privately that Alex Stewart had gone to J.B. Uniacke and suggested he "get into the boat with Johnston and the Baptists and throw Howe overboard." Uniacke, who had lately grown impatient with the intrigues of the Tory councillors, lost the last of his respect for his old party. It was reported that he had gone to the Governor and warned His Lordship that the Johnston-Stewart party was attempting to bring in a Tory party government. Whether or not the story was true, the rumour swept all over town and was never contradicted. Certainly from that time, Uniacke was a Liberal in all but name.

To make matters worse, Will Annand moved in the House that all grants to church colleges should be refused and the money given to one good college free of sectarian control and open to all denominations. Joe warmly supported the motion and, since Baptist *Acadia* had recently applied for a grant, it was at once assumed that the motion was an attack on that college. Johnston, a member of the Board of Directors of *Acadia*, stood forth as her champion, while Howe took the non-sectarian side.

It was perhaps inevitable that these two would collide. Both were men of strong views and principles, both were men of liberal minds and high intelligence, but in all other ways they were opposites. Johnston, the Tory aristocrat, was a cool and subtle man. Howe, the man of the people, was often ruled by his emotions. Johnston never permitted himself any activity which might lead to scandal and was unapproachable to the man in the street, whereas Joe Howe loved and was loved by people of all degrees, and his familiar way with women gave his enemies a useful handle against him. Johnston was a faithful adherent of the Baptist church and attended it regularly. Howe was a very irregular member of St. Matthews and attended churches of other faiths when he felt like it, his Sandemanian background leading him to distrust any leaning on creed or outward form of religion.

So Johnston went about the country all that summer with his "bevy of ministers" as Joe called them, from *Acadia*, attacking Annand's motion, while Howe dashed from town to town defending it. Soon the people were drawn into the quarrel and chose sides. Howe's argument was that, with thirty thousand children in the province needing schools to teach them basic reading, writing and arithmetic skills, the government ought to refuse money to five church colleges which served only about eighty students altogether. He did not, he said, object to churches running colleges, so long as they didn't charge them on the whole community. Johnston on his side claimed that a non-sectarian college would naturally be an ungodly one, and that *Acadia*, a child of Providence, ought to be cherished and supported.

"The mackerel," cried Joe mischievously, "run as freely into a Catholic's net or a Baptist's net as into any other, and I naturally ask myself why, as a legislator, I should make distinctions which God in His own good providence has not." This drew laughter, but soon it was no laughing matter to the Liberals. Formerly loyal Baptists broke away indignantly, weakening the party still further, and Joe's friends grew alarmed. "Take care, Howe," said Annand anxiously, "or you'll ruin everything."

Lord Falkland too was upset by the quarrel. He thought both his advisers ought to put aside their differences and pay more attention to the troubles he was having over the Casual Revenues. Howe, as Minister of Excise and Impost, had had to tell him that, for the first time in memory, the Casual Revenues had run out and there was no money to pay government salaries. He had then gone off to lock swords with Johnston over the College Question, leaving the Governor and his staff to deal with the problem. So when Joe at last found time to visit Government House, His Lordship gave him a somewhat chilly greeting. He said he had written London to ask what he must do about the salaries and had been told to apply to the Assembly.

"Apply to the Assembly," exclaimed Falkland bitterly, "when its Members have been trying for years to get control of those same Casual Revenues. Naturally they refused to hand over a penny. Now what shall I do?"

Joe saw the opening and used it. "If we had more Liberals on the Executive, sir, the Assembly might feel more generous."

"You know how hard we've tried to get Huntington."

"I could try again."

The handsome face took on a sour expression. "I fear it would be a waste of time. I could ask Lord Stanley for a parliamentary grant, I suppose, but I'm certain such a request will be refused. I thought you would surely have something original to suggest." There was a hint of sarcasm in the remark and Joe heard it.

"You might ask Lord Stanley, sir, to reopen the Civil List question," he suggested. In other words, the government could try to work out a new agreement with the Assembly by which the House would gain control of the Casual Revenues in return for paying fair salaries to officers.

"I suppose so," Lord Falkland said discontentedly. "But Lord Stanley is sure to see it as another attempt to bring in party government. He seems to fear it as he fears the devil. Yet he has only to look at Canada to see what is sure to happen here eventually, and so I told him in my last dispatch." In Canada, French and English Reformers had combined to force five Tories out of their Executive, replacing them with Liberals, thus giving the Liberal party a majority. Governor General Bagot had had to approve their action or be faced with a "No Confidence" vote which might destroy his government.

"The Canadians are moving a little too fast," Joe said with a frown. "Exchange of power, it seems to me, should take place more gradually, without harm to either party. Personally, for example, I should like to see full responsible government brought in without displacing a single Nova Scotian from office. It could be managed, too, if –" but the governor, his mind running on a different track, brushed the words aside.

"Bagot's retirement may change things," he said. "I have it on good authority that Sir Charles Metcalfe will be sent up

133

from Jamaica to take over. I know Metcalfe personally." He added, with warm approval "he won't let himself be bullied as Bagot was. He won't allow the governor's position to become little more than that of a recording clerk for the Assembly, a mere cipher!"

"I never thought of Sir Charge Bagot as a cipher," Joe began, and then, startled, realized what the Governor had just revealed. He felt a qualm of uneasiness. What lay behind Falkland's sudden concern for viceregal power? That touchy pride of his? Probably. "No governor need become a cipher under responsible government," Joe went on slowly. "He can have great influence simply as a mediator, more so I think than if he lets himself be drawn into actively taking sides."

"Do you think so," Lord Falkland said rather coldly, and changed the subject. Again, Joe felt uneasiness. Had it been unwise to speak so confidently of a governor's duties? Was Lord Falkland beginning to resent the role of pupil to adviser, one who had too confident a way, perhaps, of voicing his own opinions and, worse, one who was generally right in those opinions?

"Meanwhile," Lord Falkland said briskly, "I want you to do all you can to keep the coalition going, at least until the Whigs return to power at Home."

What else had he been doing for the past two years, Joe gloomily asked himself as he left Government House. To keep the coalition going, he had sold his paper, thrown away a good living. In order to spend more time working for the country, he had turned his back on the pleasures of family life and left Susan Ann to bear most of its burdens alone. By agreeing to join the Executive, he had allowed his party to be split and weakened. He had given up the Speakership on being appointed to ministerial office though no one had suggested he should, simply because, by the rules of responsible government, no man should hold two salaried jobs in government at one time, and he had wanted to set a good example. That extra money would have come in handy, he thought with a sigh.

What more could he do for the coalition?

End it, perhaps?

It would mean breaking his promise to Lord Sydenham. But Lord Sydenham was dead. Surely if he were alive, he would see the hopelessness of going on without party strength or support and without colleagues he could trust apart from McNab and possibly Uniacke. Collins and his Tory crowd were doing their best to kill the new system though lately instead of aiming at their usual targets, they had concentrated all their fire on McNab and himself. At the same time they had taken to praising Lord Falkland for a change. What did it mean? What did they expect to gain by it?

He could guess. Johnston would take note of what had happened in Canada. If the Liberals there had been able to force a nearly all-Liberal government on Sir Charles Bagot, perhaps he and Stewart with the help of the ex-councillors could force a full Tory one on Lord Falkland. The Stewart-Uniacke rumour pointed that way. Johnston had lately been urging the Executive to approve and forward to Lord Stanley a memorandum assuring him that Nova Scotia's government was resolutely opposed to party government. But what if, while railing at party government, he and Stewart were in reality doing their best to bring one in. How would he, Howe, go about it, if he were in Johnston's shoes? First, get the two Liberals out, persuade Lord Falkland to dissolve the House and call an election – no, first, if he were Johnston, he would run for election to the Assembly where he could work to strengthen the Tory party still further. Then a win at the polls would give him the power he needed. Power to do what? Continue the coalition or form a party government? One couldn't be certain.

Meanwhile what should he, Howe, be doing? He would try to keep the coalition alive, as Sydenham had wished, as Lord Falkland relied on him to do. How? His head felt muzzy with tiredness and uncertainty. What was the right thing to do in the circumstances? Stick by his duty, he supposed, but, Lord, how weary he was of it all – weary of treading on eggs, weary of watching every word he spoke for fear of betraying government secrets, knowing every time he turned his back someone might take a stab at him. No longer able to speak, write or be himself, he seemed no longer to have any identity.

That night he talked it over with Susan Ann.

"No matter what I do, the coalition grows weaker," he said, 'but Lord Falkland won't face the fact. There are only two things, as far as I can see, that might be done to save it. First, I could advise His Lordship to follow the Canadian example. He could ask for McNab's and my resignation, then let Johnston try the experiment of one-party rule. Then, in the next election, we could try to put his party out and our own in, and responsible government would be an established fact."

"And the other method?" asked Susan Ann, dismally aware that if her husband resigned his seat, he would also have to resign his office, and the Howes would again be without a regular income.

"The other way would be for Lord Falkland to choose between Johnston and me, sack the one he doesn't want and so bring peace to the council chamber. He could then bring in enough Liberals to please the assembly and they might be willing to pay the salaries. The coalition would be safe then for a while longer."

"His Lordship might choose Mr. Johnston," she said.

"He might," Joe admitted, "but then Johnston would have no choice but to continue the mixed administration, and it would still have one last chance of success." He strode nervously up and down their bedroom. The time for hoping and wishing was past. He would suggest the two courses to His Lordship at the first opportunity.

When, however, he went to Government House, he was told by the Governor's secretary that the press of affairs prevented His Lordship from granting Mr. Howe an interview at the present moment. His Lordship would summon Mr. Howe when he had free time. This was an ominous sign, Joe knew, but there was nothing to do but wait.

In the meantime news came from Canada of a crisis on patronage. The right to hand out jobs had always been the governor's privilege, though in practice it had usually been delegated to the family compacts. Any party hoping to gain or hold power wanted and needed the right to make appointments. The Canadian ministers had demanded it and been refused it

Government House, Halifax.

by Sir Charles Metcalfe, the new Governor General. All the ministers but one had then resigned. Metcalfe had promptly dissolved the House. There would be an election, probably early in the new year, and if the past was anything to go by, thought Joe, it would be accompanied by the usual violence. He redoubled his efforts to see Lord Falkland and was eventually successful.

He found the noble lord in an excited frame of mind over the developments in Canada. He barely listened to Joe's first suggestion, then turned on him. "You can suggest following the Canadian example when you see what has happened up there? Bagot should never have allowed the Liberals a virtual one-party government, and I do not intend to let the Conservatives have a one-party government in Nova Scotia! You yourself pointed out that changes must not come too quickly."

"It's nearly two years, sir," Joe protested, "since you promised to bring in more Liberals, yet our Executive still contains only McNab and me."

"That's enough for the present," Lord Falkland said sharply.

"Then why not accept my resignation and bring in some other Liberal who could work better with Mr. Johnston?"

"I don't want your resignation, or Mr. Johnston's. I want

the coalition to go on as it is. I warn you, Mr. Howe, I will not be insulted and rebuffed as Metcalfe was. He was quite right to retaliate by dismissing the House. I would do the same if anyone tried to force party government on me."

Joe was silent out of sheer amazement. His ears must be deceiving him, his tired mind misinterpreting the Governor's words.

"The coalition must continue," Falkland said. "Mr. Johnston agrees with me."

It came to Joe suddenly at the mention of Johnston. Lord Falkland had gone over to the Tories!

"Sir, facts must be faced," he cried urgently. "The coalition is doomed whatever happens. It can't go on as it is. There is more required to make a strong administration than nine men treating each other courteously at a round table. There should be an assurance of good faith towards each other, common sentiments and kindly feelings –"

"As between members of a political party?" interrupted His Lordship with a smile that was almost a sneer.

"Yes! You said yourself, sir, party government must come soon."

The viceregal temper erupted. "Rather than have party government here," he shouted, "I'd dissolve the House."

"Dissolve a friendly House?" Joe thought of the nearly superhuman efforts he and McNab had made during three trying Sessions to keep the Assembly even mildly sweet toward the administration. "It would be the gravest act of folly!"

The Governor's eyes grew remote.

"Thank you, Mr. Howe," he said icily, "for your advice. I intend to keep the coalition in operation until the next election at least. Then, if the people show they want party government, I shall see my duty. That will be all." He extended his hand to the bell-pull. There was nothing for Joe to do but bow and retire.

He walked slowly home by a roundabout route to avoid meeting anyone he knew and having to talk. He felt utterly shocked and miserable. He could hardly believe that the cold, furious young man in Government House was the same smiling companion of two years ago, the man he had thought of almost as a brother. That angry stranger was not the same man who had come to the Howe's home last year to offer help and sympathy in a sad time of family sorrow. Joe looked back in wonder over the past two years, when he had exerted every nerve to make Lord Falkland's administration what he called "a bright page in history."

That evening he went to see Huntington and told him the whole story.

"Johnston and Stewart are behind His Lordship," Huntington said grimly. "That's plain enough. Johnston has played on Falkland's pride of governorship and on his fears of what may happen if he angers Lord Stanley. The Tories know how weak we are now and hope to force an early election. You must resign, Howe, at once."

Joe thought about it, but finally shook his head. "I'd like to, believe me," he said wearily. "But His Lordship has promised to keep the coalition going until after the election next year. Then if the people show they want party government, he will give his approval. Meanwhile if we do anything to force it upon him – and he seems to think we'd be doing that if we resigned – he will dissolve the House at once."

Huntington caught his breath. "We can't have that," he said. "not now, with our party weaker than it's ever been before."

Joe nodded. "So you see we must keep the rickety machine going another twelve months. After that – we'll see."

A week later, on his way home from a speaking tour on the College Question, Joe was met at the Twelve Mile House by a Halifax man who, on seeing him, burst out without a word of greeting –

"Get ready for an election, Howe! Falkland's dissolved the House!"

CHAPTER THIRTEEN
1843-1848

"Two parties appeal to you for your suffrage."

Novascotian, May 17, 1847

He and McNab went into the subsequent election without joy. For nearly three years they had been asking the people to support a mixed government. Now they must turn about without any preparation and tell them the coalition was a mistake. All was upside down. Here was the remnant of the old family compact urging the people to vote for a coalition and here was Howe, who had always spoken against party, asking them to vote for a party government!

Both men won their seats. So did Johnston. They would have to wait a month, until the House met, and the Members could vote on some question of importance, to find out which party had the majority.

It worried Susan Ann that Lord Falkland had turned against his Liberal minister and was now supporting Johnston, but Joe reassured her – "It's just politics. It will pass. Lord Falkland would never be unkind."

On December 21, less than a month after the election, without waiting for a vote or talking the matter over with his Liberal ministers, Lord Falkland appointed to the vacant seat on the Executive a man named Mather Almon, Johnston's brother-in-law and a Tory of Tories. When they had recovered from the shock of the news, Joe and McNab went to Government House to ask for an explanation. "The results of the election indicated to me," Lord Falkland said coolly, "that the people are averse to party government. By choosing a man openly in favour of coalition, I show the people that I also am opposed to it. Then, too" – he fixed Howe with an unfriendly eye – "because of Mr. Almon's relationship to Mr. Johnston, *the leader of my government*, it will show the people I have perfect confidence in that gentleman." Joe and McNab resigned. So did Uniacke. Uniacke, moreover, crossed the floor to join the sadly-depleted Reform party.

The first Session of 1844 met in February and in his opening address, Lord Falkland denounced party government. This provided the necessary issue, and a debate began which lasted a fortnight. When the votes were counted, Johnston and his supporters had a majority of one, but the governor's triumph was short-lived. He invited three Liberals to take the place of the three who had resigned and the invitations were refused. His Lordship saw, with sudden alarm, that if he invited Conservatives to take the seats, he would have party government after all. He was therefore obliged to ask the three original councillors to return, but under unacceptable conditions, and when they too refused, he sat down and wrote an angry letter to the newspapers accusing the three of deliberately forcing party government on him. They replied with respect that they had done no such thing.

Joe still regarded Lord Falkland more with sorrow than anger at this time, but when, shortly after, he discovered that the Governor had sent home to England false reports of himself and his fellow Liberals, he experienced complete revulsion, and announced to a shocked country that if this system of libelling respectable colonists, who had no way of defending themselves, was continued "some colonist will by and by, or I am much mistaken, hire a black fellow to horsewhip a lieutenant-governor." After that it was, as the Governor himself said "war to the knife between himself and Howe."

With a Tory party in the majority, but with three vacant seats on the Executive, the final struggle for responsible government now began. Governor and Conservatives had the stronger forces. They were a large and wealthy group led by an astute and clever lawyer, with the colonial office solidly behind them. The Liberals were poorer men, led by a penniless ex-printer, a man with seven children, no savings and a mountain of debt. Worse, the party was split, its supporters bewildered and half-hearted.

In the emergency the party, aware that it could not go far without Howe, raised a sum of money to give to him which partly made up for the income he had lost by resigning office. Falkland's press later taunted him for accepting the money and called him a place-hunter. In reply, Joe reminded Lord Falkland that he, Howe, had served his sovereign for nothing for two years while His Lordship was receiving seven thousand pounds from the government. "You have held places for many years," wrote Joe, "how won I know not; but the public services by which they were obtained are yet to be recorded." Bitterly must Falkland have regretted his kindly condescension to that vulgar printer Howe, "associate of Indians, innkeepers and other low fellows."

"Falkland is still as obstinate as a mule," Joe wrote his sister around this time, "and the Tories as savage as devils, and they may still have the majority of one or two, but for all these I care not, but I would have cared if they had got the people too. It would have broken my heart, after spending the flower of my days in teaching them and throwing away my living to set them an example, to find them giving me up for any lord in Christendom." He referred to the sorrows of the past year, in his home and in hers. "The world has not known, but I may confess it to you, that the scenes of the previous year were not the right preparation for those through which I have had to fight my way of late. They have weighed upon my spirit like lead, often when my utmost buoyancy was required." But with a two-year battle ahead of him to win back what the Liberal party had lost, Joe had little time to think of the past.

In fact, he was experiencing freedom again and it was a glorious feeling. Will Annand, owner of both the *Novascotian* and a new daily, the *Chronicle*, had handed over the editorship of both papers, and Joe was happier than he had been in many months. His vibrant voice rang out once again over all the land –

"Nova Scotians! The irresponsible rule of Toryism is again fastened upon you. Your old enemies are in possession of the Citadel and you must dislodge them!"

Meanwhile Lord Falkland went rushing about the country making speeches, like a politician running for office. Heedless of his dignity, he talked to largely unresponsive audiences about "that crafty Howe" and referred to party government as "an instrument of mischief." His heart was now bleeding for the ex-councillors and their friends. He said they might suffer so much from Liberal domination if the Liberals got into power, the poor fellows might have to leave the country.

Joe on his side soon had the whole country laughing at the electioneering Lord, and the furious Governor could only fight back by proscribing him, that is, by condemning him without trial as "a dangerous man who wrote in the newspapers, making fun of authority." Tory leader Johnston took up the cudgels on the Governor's behalf by condemning Joe's set of joke verses beginning "The Lord of the Bed-Chamber sat in his shirt" as indecent. Joe replied from the floor of the House that it was the first time he had ever suspected it was a grave offense to hint that a nobleman wore a shirt, one to be prosecuted in the high court of parliament by an Attorney General. "It is a trifle to damn a Nova Scotian's character but an unpardonable offence to hint that a nobleman wears a shirt." Lord Falkland stuck it out to the end of his term and then asked to be transferred. He left the colony without tears on either side.

Joe set out in earnest now to regain his hold on the country. He spoke at meetings and picnics. Once again he caught and held the imagination of the people. He had a way of throwing back his coat before he began to speak, which was like a challenge and a promise. He usually started with a joke. "The history of wine is curious; its invention is attributed to Noah, who certainly had seen enough of the evils of water." When he had his audience laughing and relaxed, then he would settle down to deliver a speech especially designed for the people listening and quite unlike the one delivered at the stop before. Here he is speaking to the black people of Preston about land grants, long denied them by the family compact.

"And when did you get them? When that great scoundrel Joe Howe got into the council and for the first time acquired executive influence. One of our first acts was to obtain for you, free of cost, one general grant confirming your titles. You remember the day when I came here with the grant in my hand?"

"We remember, we remember," cried his audience.

"Again my friends, during all the thirty-six years you have lived in Nova Scotia, did you ever hear of a coloured man being on a jury until the year before last?"

"Never!"

"Well, you see coloured people on juries now. Tell the Tories that when they bother you again."

"We will. We will."

By the spring of 1845, he was badly in need of a rest and moved his family to Annand's farm at Musquodoboit, where they lived for most of two years. "They were the happiest two years of my life," he always claimed. Like his neighbours, he pitched hay, ploughed, reaped and cradled. "I had been for a long time over-working my brains and under-working my body. Here I worked my body and rested my brains." He read to his children in the evenings and spent much time in the quiet woods. Country folk are inclined to be suspicious of the town dweller, so it speaks well for Joe Howe that throughout his long life the Musquodoboit people were always his most faithful supporters. Working beside him day by day, they came to know him. They listened to his political views and in turn instructed him in country life. They could laugh at him sometimes too, like the time he came home from the woods with a pet for his little girls. "You may know a lot about government, Howe," they chuckled, "but you sure don't know about skunks," and they helped him bury every stitch of the clothing he was wearing at the time.

In the last three months of 1846, Joe travelled from one end of the province to the other, attending sixty meetings in ninety days. He would be seen on countless fairgrounds, dashing about with first one lady on his arm, then another, stopping to bestow a kiss on yet another. Then he was kept busy finding seats for them all on the best benches, while the other candidates sat primly on the platform waiting to be formally introduced. During one trip, he sent a message to Susan Ann over the new telegraph – "God bless you, my darling. I have kissed about five hundred women since I left home, but I shall be glad to find myself in your arms again." The kissing was partly political, no doubt, but he found it easy and natural to express affection and nobody seemed upset by it. One very proper spinster, the daughter of old Dr. Thomas McCulloch of Pictou in fact, was heard to *boast* that Mr. Howe had chased her three times around a ship's deck to give her a kiss.

He was at ease with everyone. Seeing a man he knew – black, white, Indian – he would link an arm in his, call him by his first name and ask about his wife or inquire about the health of his baby. Old men who had known him from the start of his career seemed to idolize him. One old fellow, meeting him just before the election, earnestly apologized for his sons not having voted for him at the previous election. "If only I'd had the least suspicion that my boys would so betray me, Mr. Howe, I should never have had anything to do with bringing the ingrates into the world!" George Johnson tells of seeing him once talking to an old man, a supporter of his in Annapolis County, and on rising to go, Howe kissed the old face and asked God to bless his few remaining years. "I saw great tears roll down the old man's face, and I knew then why it was that the people loved Joe Howe."

He always enjoyed the speech-making and the quips that flew back and forth during the question period. He stayed for the parties afterwards which usually lasted till midnight, and never missed a dance. Then it was back to Halifax to taunt the Tories in the House for their lack of initiative. Naturally enough, Johnston was unwilling to risk his frail majority by introducing unpopular resolutions. He was still short three members of

145

Council and had to stand plenty of ridicule from Howe on that score too. "We are told that the Attorney-General deserves a monument for opposing this bill. Should Mr. Johnston depart this life, I have no objection to the monument provided it tells the truth – 'Here lies the man who denounced party government that he might form one, and, professing justice to all parties, gave every office to his own.'"

Province House was like a theatre when Howe spoke. Everyone laughed and applauded, while the perspiring sergeant-at-arms kept shouting "Order! Order!" without the least effect. The pace picked up as election day approached. The number of buttonholes sporting blue bellflowers (they are still called "Joe Howes" in parts of Nova Scotia) grew more numerous, but the Tories too were outdoing themselves. With all the patronage of government at their disposal and the funds of some of the colony's richest men, they stood a good chance of winning. "Will you stand by your Queen's representative in upholding Her Majesty's supremacy?" they thundered, "or join Howe and Uniacke in what the *New York Express* pithily calls 'the struggle of 1776.' Abandon a party which cares not a straw about the British connection, who consistently wish that Nova Scotia were a state of the Union."

The Tories paid large sums of money openly into the bank to buy support. Perhaps the Liberals did the same when they could afford it, but chiefly they depended on the magic of Joe's tongue. He wrote Charles Buller, the colonial Reformer, that he had spoken five hours the day before and had replied to eleven speeches later in the debate. "It was hard work, but rare fun." Buller on his side sent cheering news from England: "The Corn Laws are sure to be repealed," he wrote, "which will remove one of the main reasons, trade, for keeping the colonies in subjection. Now that the Whigs are in again, with Lord Grey as Colonial Secretary, you will see a new spirit in the country."

His estimate of the situation was correct. When Sir John Harvey came to take Lord Falkland's place, one of his first acts was to send a note to Mr. Howe, inviting him to Government

House, from which Joe had been barred by proscription for two years.

As always, Joe kept his sister Jane informed. "The rising of the people is like the rising of the Nile. You may calculate upon both with some degree of faith. Since last March, I have been like a person in a sea-fight all the time, smothered in the smoke and deafened with the roar of battle. Now my countrymen are with me and for aught else I care not, with me as unanimously and affectionately as in 1838 or 1840, and they are conducting themselves with a spirit and intelligence which will entitle them still to rank in advance of all British Americans. The waters have risen," he closed exuberantly, "and there will be corn in Egypt yet!"

In May, he addressed a letter to the Freeholders. "I have never known you wanting in the hour of trial," he wrote proudly, "and I never knew a case in which the lines of distinction between parties to a controversy were more clear and unmistakeable than in this. If you falter now, with the enemy before you, with the fruits of victory within your grasp, the highest privileges of British subjects to be cast away by a single act in a single day, I shall cease to labour because I shall cease to hope." He had brought them along thus far, these Scots, Irish, English, Germans, New Englanders and Acadians of Nova Scotia, taught them, lectured them, encouraged them, loved them. Now they must show what they could do.

They showed him.

When the House met on January 22, 1848, a vote of "No Confidence" ended one administration and installed another upon the sound principles of responsible cabinet government for the first time in any British colony in the world. Nova Scotia had been, as Joe had wished her to be, a model for the upper provinces and for all the far-flung British colonies.

It was a proud and happy day when Howe, Doyle, Uniacke, Huntington, McNab and four others entered Government House to be sworn into office. For Joe the beautiful stone mansion held memories – of his Post Office errands to the back door when he was a boy, of his interview that morning ten years ago with Sir Colin Campbell, and later on, of his famous meeting with Lord Sydenham.

But for Joe this was not an ending, but a beginning. Even before responsible government had been won, he had been busy designing a concept far grander than colonial self-rule – a plan for Imperial Federation.

CHAPTER FOURTEEN
1848-1850

*"We must be Britons in every inspiring sense
of the word."*

Speeches and Letters, Volume II

"Now, dear," said Susan Ann with faint hope, "you can take things a little easier."

The Honourable Joseph Howe, Provincial Secretary of Nova Scotia, looked at his wife across the breakfast table with astonishment. "Take things easier? My dear girl, this is just a start." He got up from the table a picture of energy and determination. The tawny hair and eyebrows showed traces of grey, but at forty-four he was still vigorous, and his mouth had kept its humour and generosity. "All we've got so far is control over our domestic affairs."

She had no right to feel surprised. She knew her husband, and was aware of his reaching ambition. As long as two years ago, she had looked over his shoulder as he wrote to Lord John Russell, pleading with him to make wider use of the abilities of colonists. "The Boston boy may become president of the United States. The young native of Halifax or Quebec can never be anything but the member of an Executive Council." Why not, he had asked, employ capable British North Americans in the colonial office, for who should know more about such matters than a colonial? But Lord John Russell had so far made no move to do so.

"At the moment," Joe told his wife, "everyone's delighted. They've got responsible government. They'll soon have new roads and bridges, lighthouses, better education facilities, possibly at less expense. But that's *all* they can expect. They know their Members can't do a thing about our high postal rates, our injurious trade tariffs, our immigration policies. Britain still controls our trade."

She protested that Britain would surely not do anything purposely to injure their trade. He raised an eyebrow. "Not so long ago, if you remember, England called a halt to protection, and we suddenly had to scurry around and find new customers for our fish and lumber. I'm for free trade, as you know, but I resent the fact that we had no say in that matter. At this very moment, Susan Ann, British statesmen are meeting the Americans to discuss a commercial treaty which will affect the trade of all the British provinces. Britain may bargain away our fisheries to gain some small advantage for herself or for Canada – and thus ruin Nova Scotia's economy. But are we represented at that negotiation table? We are not. We won't even be consulted."

Susan Ann listened with mournful understanding.

"And what of war-making?" Joe's voice grew more indignant. "Does Britain ever ask us if we want war? What if she opens hostilities with our neighbour as she did in 1812? Our country becomes the battlefield and we have nothing to say about it. We don't even have an ambassador in London. Why not? Because we are considered mere colonials – inferior Britons!" He brought the problem closer home: "Here's young Joe talking already of a career in the navy. We know how little chance he has of ever getting a commission." He thought of his own career. Forty-four years old, with more than twenty active years in politics, yet apart from the premiership, he had reached the pinnacle of a colonial's ambition.

"I don't envy the Americans their country, their climate, or their wealth," he cried with passion. "What I do envy them is their great field of honourable competition. The poorest man in the smallest state may win the highest national honours, even become President. And that's the difference between us. The sons of the rebels are men full-grown, the sons of the Loyalists are not." He took a deep breath. "Do you know,

James W. Johnston (1792-1873) lawyer, Chief Justice of Nova Scotia, leader of the Tories, and Joe Howe's main opponent for many years.

Susie, what I'd do if I could work myself into a position of prominence in Britain?"

She looked at him wonderingly.

"I'd urge Parliament to let colonials sit in the British House of Commons and help rule the Empire!"

"They'd think you mad!"

"Twenty years ago people thought Robert Baldwin with his responsible nonsense mad. Twenty years ago, the Pictou Scribblers and a few others of us were considered not only mad, but disloyal. Yet today we have responsible government."

"But, Joseph, if all the representatives of all the forty colonies went to sit in the House of Commons, it would have to sit for a year."

He agreed this was true. "But not all the colonies would send representatives, only those with responsible government. And there need be only one or two from each. I haven't worked it all out yet, but the basic idea, as I see it, is for all of us to work together, helping each other and giving sound advice to the Queen, so that at last we would have an Empire so powerful, so prosperous in peace, so invincible in war, that future wars would be most unlikely. Who would dare declare one against so great a federation?"

Susan Ann may not have wholly shared his enthusiasm but she did know that argument from her would have little effect. Her faint hope of his taking things easier had already faded. Joseph must always be doing, always be fighting and finding out. "How do you hope to gain this prominent position in Britain?"

"By doing my job so well here," he said, eyes alight under the arrogant brows, "that British statesmen will be bound to offer me an Imperial appointment. Once I am working for Britain, I shall be in a position to place my plan before the proper authorities."

Not long after this, Howe and Johnston found themselves on the same side. The Reciprocity Treaty, designed to regulate trade between the British American provinces and the United States for a period of ten years, had just been signed at Washington. What both men resented was the fact that Lord Elgin, the Queen's representative, had signed for all the provinces and that Nova Scotia had not been represented at the bargaining table. As a result, the Americans had been given the right to dry and cure fish on the Nova Scotian coast without being required to give the same rights to Nova Scotia on theirs.

The suggestions of Howe and Johnston for righting this injustice, however, were quite different.

Johnston moved that the House consider the possibility of a confederation of all the British American provinces as a protection against such cavalier treatment by the Home government in future.

Joe opposed the motion on the ground that a better method would be Imperial federation. "Talk of a union of the provinces," he said with ringing scorn. "What we need is union with the Empire!" He argued that Nova Scotia would be just as much at a disadvantage with provincial union as she was now: "Is it not possible that the farmers of western Canada, in their anxiety to get their wheat into the United States, might throw our fisheries overboard?" In any case, he insisted, before they could even think of such a political union, they must have a physical one – the intercolonial railway.

He succeeded in defeating Johnston's motion, and he had officially planted in the House the seed of his plan – but the seed of Confederation had been planted too.

Meanwhile the proposed intercolonial railroad provided Joe with his first opportunity to make a reputation for himself in Britain. Railroads by this time were in the front of everyone's mind. This exciting new mode of travel would soon change the whole face of the country, open the wilderness to settlement, make some men richer, others poorer. It would draw the provinces together through trade and make them stronger, better able to face any American aspirations at the border.

There were already short lines from Toronto and Montreal to American cities but what was most needed was a line connecting Canada with the Maritimes for reasons of trade and also in case of war. Railways, however, were costly. Canada had already been refused British aid to build an intercolonial line, and Nova Scotia could only afford to construct a short line within the province and was doing so when, in August of 1850, the people of Portland, Maine, wrote asking her to join them in building a line from the border to Halifax through New Brunswick. Nova Scotia sent delegates to the convention at Portland and in the following month a public meeting to hear their report was held in Temperance Hall.

The first enthusiasm was dashed when it was learned that Nova Scotia would need to raise nearly a million dollars as her share. At this point, the Provincial Secretary asked if he might address the meeting.

"The floor is yours, Mr. Howe."

Did they, Joe asked, really want the Americans to come in and build their railroad? Should it not be built by Nova Scotians and owned by Nova Scotians? Should not railways be like ordinary roads, public highways which would always belong to the people? Railroad promoters in Portland were not interested in Nova Scotia, only in profits. "Why pay some private capitalist a million dollars, when by applying to Britain for a loan at a low rate of interest we can do the work ourselves and more cheaply? Let Nova Scotia's government assume the whole responsibility, pledge public revenues, borrow the money honestly, and spend it honestly on the people's behalf." The audience applauded wildly and Tories, who had not spoken to Joe for years, came up and shook his hand. Huntington, and Johnston were opposed, however, saying they thought government should not be entrusted with such dangerous and costly experiments. It was decided, nevertheless, to apply to the Mother Country for a loan, or the guarantee of one. Britain's reply to the request was that a railway to Maine would be an excellent plan, but she could provide no money for the purpose at this time. Angry and disappointed, the Nova Scotians asked themselves why it was that the Home government could loan large sums at reasonable interest rates to rebellious Canada for canals, and even to the United States, but not to the loyal colony of Nova Scotia.

"We must refuse to take 'No' for an answer," said Joseph Howe firmly.

So the House of Assembly made him a committee-of-one to go to London and try to change the minds of the Prime Minister and Parliament. Pleased with the opportunity and seeing it as a challenge, possibly the first step towards that position of prominence in England, Joe sailed for Liverpool. He kept a journal during this railway mission. Reading it, one sees that much of his self-confidence was assumed. "When I found myself in the heart of London, with its ten millions of people around me, of whom I knew not ten, I felt that if I ventured to raise my voice at all, I'd resemble the man howling in the wilderness."

How was he to persuade Lord Grey of the colonial office that Nova Scotia needed a line through New Brunswick to connect with the American road at the border and then to ask Parliament, on Nova Scotia's behalf, to give, or guarantee, a loan of nearly a million pounds for the purpose?

CHAPTER FIFTEEN
1850-1851

"I regard these railroads, after all, but as means for the accomplishment of elevated and beneficent ends."

Speeches and Letters II, 59-74

In his modest lodgings in Sloane Street, Joe Howe sat down and wrote a letter to Lord Grey, making his formal application and asking for an interview. Reading it over, he saw that his request was clearly argued and mildly eloquent. Finding no way to improve it, he went out and put the letter in the box. Then, because it was a Sunday and one too fine to spend indoors, he strolled across the Square and along King's Road until he came to a church where, on impulse, he went in, still thinking of his letter. Presently the sermon caught his attention and for an hour he forgot all about railroads.

He came out, soothed by the choral music, and walked slowly through Green Park where crowds of Londoners had been lured out by the unseasonably fine weather. Suddenly, between one step and another, came one of his "flashes." Words seemed to leap out of the air at him – emigration! colonization! commerce! Clear out the slums, send England's paupers to the empty lands of America, bring back representatives to the House of Commons! As one thought crowded on another, his stride lengthened excitedly. Here were good solid reasons why, not only a Portland branch but an intercolonial line as well, would be as useful to Britain as to Nova Scotia! If all the colonies would pledge land and money to secure Britain against loss, the provinces could have their intercolonial railway, Britain would get North American customers for her goods, and the paupers of England would get new homes and jobs on the railroad. Best of all, it could turn his dream of Imperial federation into something concrete.

Rocked by the possibilities, Joe went next morning to the British Museum and for a week looked up everything written on emigration, colonization, and railways. Then, confident that his facts and figures were accurate and up to date, he sat down and wrote a second letter to Lord Grey. It ran to ten thousand words and was a remarkable piece of writing. At one moment he writes with tactful humility: "In offering suggestions to the ministers of the Crown, I feel, my Lord, the distance which divides me in rank and intelligence from those I would presume to counsel" and at the next he is accusing Britain of negligence, of keeping the British provinces in a state of inferiority, warning His Lordship that Britain will lose the other half of the North American continent if she is not careful.

"British statesmen," he wrote bluntly, "have so far lacked the courage or energy to deal with their own extensive poverty and crime in a practical way." Yet the colonies of British North American needed only to be linked by railroads to provide a vast new territory for emigration. "We will combine our surplus land with your surplus labour for our mutual advantage, that the poor may be fed, the waste places filled up, and this great Empire strengthened and preserved."

He wrote sixty foolscap pages at a stretch, working steadily all day and half the night. In the next few days he corrected and copied them, thinking of nothing else. Surely this letter would strengthen his game for the railroad stakes, unless of course it offended by its boldness. That risk must be taken. The letter was dispatched.

That done, Howe set to work in another direction. He looked to see what other chances of a loan existed in London in case the government turned him down. Of the several companies he saw, one was the contracting firm of Jackson, Peto, Betts and Brassey, two of whose partners were Members of the British Parliament. He had several personal meetings with their North American representative, Charles Archibald, a former

Nova Scotian, but in the end the company said it was not prepared to undertake such a financial risk. All his hopes, therefore, had to wait on the decision of Parliament.

After ten anxious days, he received a reply from Lord Grey. "I have received your letter of the fourth and I have read it with the attention which its great importance deserves." Great importance! "Come now," he exults in his diary, "that's pretty good from a minister of state to a poor Bluenose far away from his friends in the big city." His flash had been light from heaven. Lord Grey had questioned some minor points in his plan, so the following day Joe sat down and answered the objections in a second letter. His next task was to talk with people who might be in a position to persuade Members of Parliament to vote for Nova Scotia's application. Gradually, with the help of the few people he knew and with introductions to this man and that, he enlarged his circle of friends and began to spread over London the gospel of railroads and colonization. His confidence grew. If the British government turned him down, he thought cockily, I'll appeal to the people.

A fortnight later, his conceit was shattered. An official letter came from Under-Secretary Hawes; it was a flat, cold refusal. A day was set for his interview, as promised, but Hawes made it clear it would be a brief one, simply a formality. It was a bitter blow to Joe and it came when he was ill with a bad cold and heavy congestion of the lungs. "My voice has been gone for a month," he wrote, "and my lungs are dreadfully oppressed, not in good trim to fight an Imperial government and agitate England."

Two days later, he received a message from the mayor of Southampton asking if he would come down there and address the citizens of the town. "Will I!" Howe shouts in his journal. This was the sort of thing he had prayed for, a hustings from which to arouse public interest in his scheme and thus influence the House of Commons. Of course, if next day the Colonial Secretary stood by his letter of refusal, the invitation from Southampton would have come too late. Joe set out next morning for the interview in a mood of do or die.

After the usual long wait on one of the shabby chairs of the anteroom, he heard his name called and jumped to his feet. Marching across the threshold of the inner office, he saw Lord Grey and Hawes standing together by the window in deep conversation, a hint perhaps that the interview must not be of long duration. As they turned to him, polite but distant, Joe was saying grimly to himself – "Two to one and long odds, but here goes 'ye cogging Greeks,' have at ye both!"

"When I entered the room," he wrote Susan Ann that evening, "everything I hoped for trembled in the balance. When I came out two hours later, Hawes had the 'refusal letter' in his pocket and it was to be struck off the files. I had permission to go on in my own way and finish my case before any decision was given. I have, besides, a general assurance of sympathy and aid, and permission to feel the pulse of the public in any way I please. Viva! 'Boldness in civic business' as old Bacon says. But, as I go down Downing Street, my heart is too full of thankfulness to leave much room for triumph."

He set off in the stage for Southampton a few days later, his voice almost as good as new, ready to "feel the pulse of the public." He prayed he would be equal to the task.

When Joe Howe of Nova Scotia – a little-known politician from an almost unknown colony – rose to address the people of England for the first time, he began by taking them into his confidence, telling them in a homely, natural way how he had once visited Southampton as a colonial tourist but had never dreamed he would return to address such an audience within its ancient walls. He led them skilfully by praise of their historic town to his main theme, the wish to draw closer the ties of affection between British North America and the Mother Country, "to reproduce England on the far side of the Atlantic," and to ease the shocking conditions under which so many poor folk lived in the crowded cities of England. He offered concrete plans, arguments, statistics, and showed what part the railroad would play in them. Then, as always when he spoke of something he felt deeply, the magic came. Warmth and passion poured forth in vivid, rhythmic language, and his audience hung on every word. For the first time, his plea for Imperial federation was heard by an audience beyond the borders of Nova Scotia.

"Before the American revolution," he said, "the old philosopher, Benjamin Franklin, came over to this country on a mission which failed. The government of that day treated him coldly, but he forgot to appeal to the people. I believe that if the people of this country had understood the question then as they do now, much bloodshed and expenditure would have been saved. In the British people I have an abiding faith –" an outburst of clapping stopped him for a moment. "During the old times of persecution," he went on, "four brothers bearing my name left the southern counties of England and settled in four of the old New England states. Their descendants number thousands and are scattered from Maine to California. My father," he said with pride, "was the only descendant of that stock who, at the Revolution, adhered to the side of England. I am his only surviving son; and whatever the future may have in store, I want when I stand beside his grave to feel that I have done my best to preserve the connection he valued, that the British flag may wave above the soil in which he sleeps." He thanked them and sat down. There was a moment's dead silence. Then came the applause, and it went on and on, like waves pounding on the shore. My little country, thought Joe, bless her snow-clad hills, will be more respected here in future, or I am much mistaken.

Invitations poured in afterwards to speak in other cities. News articles praised Mr. Howe's "lucid reasoning, his profound political philosophy and forcible eloquence" and urged the government to put his suggestions into effect at once. The speech was printed in pamphlet form and Joe saw that copies were distributed where they might do some good. His name was mentioned in the House of Lords and a question asked about him in the Commons, where his plan was praised for its boldness and originality. He received more invitations to the country houses of the great and near-great than he had time to accept. He met and dined with Charles Dickens, visited Carlyle

160

and Thackeray, and attended the Lord Mayor's Banquet and the Chelsea Arts Ball.

He was even presented to the Queen. It seems to have been a nerve-wracking business. When the moment came, Joe was so busy measuring his steps, preparing to go down gracefully on one knee without tripping over his sword, there was hardly time to experience the full flavour of the moment: "And here goes 'Bluenose' – a look – a step – and my knee is bent before my sovereign and her little hand at my lips. Before I could recover," he wrote Susan Ann, "Lord Grey springs at me, seizes my hand, and in a moment I am shaking hands with Johnny Russell and chatting with the great head of the Whigs." It was all wonderful and a great triumph, and Joe enjoyed himself hugely.

Nevertheless that four-month stay in England was, on the whole, a trying one. Just as Lord Grey began to show interest and when, in fact, Joe had his private assurance the guarantee would be given, the Whigs were suddenly turned out of office and Joe's work had all to be done over with a new Colonial Secretary. Luckily, in less than a fortnight, the Tories in their turn were defeated and Grey was back in office.

On March 10, Joe received Hawes' letter, pledging the guarantee for the loan.

"Dispatch at last," he wrote thankfully. "Read it in bed. Laid my head down and thanked God, who had crowned all my labours with such success. My solitary thoughts, hopes, fears, toils, and trials, He only knows or can know. Five months seem like a dream. Thank God with all my heart and soul for His mercies."

He mailed the precious letter home to the Provincial Secretary with his report, a copy of which he sent to the colonial office, and then he boarded the next steamer for home. "How should I have felt returning mortified and unsuccessful. The very thought of the risks I ran makes me quiver. Successful beyond my own, beyond anybody's hopes." He had been sent to England to ask for one railroad and had got two, to ask for a million pounds and he had got seven million!

On top of all that, he had made his name a household word in London. Prospects looked bright for Imperial federation.

Because Lord Grey had agreed to the guarantee on condition that it benefit all three British provinces and all three must be in agreement on detail, Joe set off for Montreal and Toronto soon after he arrived home. He told officials in these cities they were to have help after all in building an intercolonial railway. "I was invested with no authority from you," he admitted, "and in speaking for you, rather than in your names, I was often compelled to assume a responsibility and to utter opinions which you might afterwards repudiate."

Audiences of both French and English Canadians loved him and were convinced. He went on to Saint John where, after a large formal dinner, he kept everyone laughing at his stories until nearly dawn, and long after the wine had run out. In Portland, an old gentleman claimed that Mr. Howe's eloquence had added years to his life – it would take that long to get over laughing at his stories. The tour became a royal progress, ending with a grand reception at Halifax, complete with fireworks.

Tired as he was, he had to plunge at once into an election campaign, leaving his safe seat in Halifax County to run in Cumberland against a young doctor named Tupper, where there was some opposition to the railroad. After the election, he went to Boston again to a mammoth railway celebration held under canvas on Boston Common. When his turn came to speak, he dwelt with tact on the recent growth of good relations between the two countries, not bowing an inch to any assumption of American superiority, but praising the country's resources, its progress, and especially its lovely womenfolk. He ended with a dig and a compliment. "You have tried once or twice, I believe, to invade our frontiers. When next you make the attempt, let me advise you to put the women of New England in the front rank and you will be sure to succeed." They laughed and applauded for minutes on end.

He came home, satisfied all was going well, that he had taken care of all the groundwork. All that remained was to get the necessary legislation passed in the House.

The first whisper of trouble came with the appearance of Charles Archibald on the scene. Nova Scotia, with seven million pounds to spend, had suddenly become interesting to his firm, Jackson, Peto, Betts and Brassey. When it was known that the company would sell stock in the undertaking, with interest (it was rumoured) at eleven per cent, many of Joe's party, as well as the Opposition, were in favour of letting the British firm build the railroad. Not Howe.

"We don't need them now," he said. "Not as co-partners, anyway. If they want to come in as contractors that's different, for I see no objection to their spending for their own and our advantage the whole seven million as long as we are in charge, that is, and keep the money in our own hands. If they come as co-partners, we shall be at their mercy. We cannot afford to take risks with the public's money."

One or two looked mutinous and he saw he would have opposition from his own share-hungry Liberals as well as the Tories, and he did. The battle of the Railway Bills was long and heated, but in the end they passed. Joe went home to Susan Ann, exhausted but content. "My countrymen have redeemed every pledge I ever gave for them," he said with pride, "at home and abroad."

Less than three weeks later, the blow fell.

It came in a dispatch to the Governor from the colonial office and was sent on to Mr. Howe, the Provincial Secretary. Reading it, Joe felt his world sway under his feet. Lord Grey wrote that Mr. Howe had misunderstood the arrangements – the guarantee applied only to the Quebec line, not to the Portland one. The Imperial guarantee would therefore have to be withdrawn.

Anyone stepping into the office at that moment would have seen a Joe Howe who had aged ten years in as many minutes.

CHAPTER SIXTEEN
1852-1863

"Talk of a Union of the Provinces ... What we require is union with the Empire!"

Speeches and Letters, 1854

For a few very bad hours, Joe believed the fault had indeed been his, that he had somehow misunderstood Lord Grey, and he expressed to the Governor his "regret and deep mortification." Inevitably, however, he began to search his memory.

In London, he had argued from start to finish that both lines were essential to British interests, yet no one had said to him then "Forget the line to Portland." In his report, a copy of which had been sent to the colonial office, the terms of the guarantee had been plainly stated. In the House he had described both propositions in unmistakeable terms, and no one had contradicted him. A copy of that speech, he recalled suddenly, had gone to Lord Grey's office. He got it out of the file and saw His Lordship's reply pinned to it: "I feel very sanguine of the ultimate assent of New Brunswick to the measure as proposed. I think all you have done about the railways very judicious and, without flattery, I may say that I do not know when I have read a better or abler speech." After writing that in June, now at the end of November His Lordship informs Mr. Howe that he misunderstood him and the guarantee was only for the trunk line through Canada.

What had happened between those two letters?

Mr. Archibald had come to Nova Scotia. This representative of the great London contractors, Jackson, Peto, Brassey and

Betts, had suggested his firm build a railroad for Nova Scotia for its own profit. Joe Howe had wanted, however, to build one at the least cost to the province and had got his way. Then what did the great contractors do? Did they, seeing a million dollars profit about to slip out of their clutches, bring pressure to bear on Lord Grey, a fellow member of the House of Commons? Did they ask him to take the guarantee away from Nova Scotia and put the money elsewhere – in Canada, for instance, or New Brunswick, where there were men in government less scrupulous about the public money and where Jackson, Peto, Brassey and Betts might get another chance at those golden guineas?

He could not prove this. He would not be allowed to try. He imagined the reaction in Canada, in New Brunswick and Portland, when they heard that Howe had naively misunderstood his instructions. After all his fine talk, he would look a fool and, quite possibly, a villain. In England, too, he would be recalled as "that poor colonial simpleton who had foolishly put his trust in the word of a British minister."

Yet all that didn't matter. He'd lived down censure and ridicule before. He would again. The terrible thing to him was how this would affect his plan to draw England and the colonies closer together, the plan which Lord Grey himself had said "would effect a change in the civilized world." The English poor would go on working ten and twelve hours a day in mines and factories for a pittance; paupers and their children would continue to live meanly in workhouses; in British North America the railroads would not be built, perhaps for years, and the country would fall still further behind its rich and energetic neighbour. All this so a few British businessmen and possibly a few "get-rich-quick" Nova Scotians and Canadians could make a few hundred pounds profit.

If he had never before seen the need for an arrangement of the Empire to prevent influential Britons from exploiting colonials, he saw it now. "What remedy had I," he asked one of his critics in Canada some years later, "when Lord Grey's dispatch shattered the noblest scheme of colonial policy ever devised?" None whatever suited to the magnitude of the wrong. Joe would have given all he was worth, or might be worth, for the opportunity to appeal from Lord Grey to the House of Commons, but such a thing was not possible.

It was Howe's most bitter learning experience. He did not give up his vision of Imperial federation, nor did his allegiance to the Mother Country falter, but he would never again be so trusting of British politicians.

From that time too, he played his country's cards closer to his chest, refusing to join the Canadians in what he felt would be a futile effort to change Lord Grey's decision. He returned instead to his original plan to build a road just for Nova Scotia. He went to England again, persuaded British bankers to loan the necessary funds at a fair rate, and in 1854 succeeded in getting new railway bills passed. He then accepted the chairmanship of the Railway Board, resigning as Provincial Secretary but holding his seat in the House. For the next two years he supervised the building of some forty-five miles of track between Halifax and Windsor Junction, with a line west to Windsor. Under his supervision, not the least whisper of bribery or corruption touched it. In New Brunswick, where Jackson, Peto, Brassey and Betts had been taken in as partners, that province had eventually to buy them out at great additional expense.

After the triumphs and disappointments of responsible government and the railroad mission, Joe spent ten active years in and out of government, never idle, always curious, always willing to tackle whatever was asked of him. As a politician, he was continually besieged by his constituents for jobs, for money, for help in tracing a lost husband, for getting a son out of jail. As Provincial Secretary, he was the friend and guide of each new governor. His only holidays were missions to England or the United States at government expense, but these he greatly enjoyed. "Travelling," he said, "gives to a man of observation, who has nerve and bodily activity, and who dives into every place where there is anything to be seen, an amount of knowledge and instruction which cannot, by those who have not gone over the same ground, be estimated or conceived."

And wherever he went, he wrote lengthy and highly-readable letters home to his wife or Jane and to his children as well. As a father, he was affectionate and fair, encouraging his five boys and two girls to act on their own initiative. In 1854, when Governor LeMarchent told him he would hold open a midshipman's berth for one of Howe's sons, this is the letter the Victorian parent wrote to his two sons, aged eleven and thirteen, both then away at school: "I cannot decide" he said, [meaning as to which boy should have the opportunity] "without your own wishes being consulted. The appointment, which makes you a midshipman at once, puts your foot on the lowest rung of the ladder, at the top of which there are the highest honours of the navy. The risks are death or loss of limb in doing your duty. Both, if you accept, bear in mind that Nelson, who feared nothing, must be your model. The pay is barely sufficient for maintenance at first and the chances of making money are not very great. Now don't both speak at once, but talk it over between yourselves. Say nothing to anybody else and, having thought well and reflected, write me what I am to do."

As it turned out, only Syd was qualified by age, and we find his father a few months later writing him from England: "Believe me, my dear boy, that my thoughts are seldom from you. Every little midshipman that I see about London reminds me of my own dear boy ... Your last letter was very well written and well expressed. Try to improve. Always do your best and then the task will soon come easy."

Howe was a man who loved children. "I have seen Mr. Howe put children on his knee and talk to them of their future," George Johnston tells us, "and there was nothing artificial about it." Out of his own eleven, Joe and his wife lost five. We find no record of his feelings on the occasion of their deaths, but we can guess them by reading one of the hundreds of letters he wrote to other parents in the same situation. Here is one written in 1871 to a man who had just lost his daughter: "The pleasures that children bring with them are manifold and engrossing, but unfortunately we feel their loss in proportion as we have loved them. There is no solace but time, and as it passes we cease to mourn and turn to the duties which cannot be put aside."

The ten years saw defeats as well as victories. His effort to recruit Americans for the Crimean War was not only fruitless, the bad feelings stirred up by it led to his defeat in 1858 by Dr. Tupper. Saddest of all was the fact that, as the years sped by, he made no progress in persuading Britain he could serve her in a wider capacity, so his plan for a federation of the British Empire lay gathering dust.

In 1860 he was in office again, this time as Premier. He had never aspired to this particular honour, the highest open to a colonial, for in that day the chief power lay in the hands of the Provincial Secretary, and he had been that from the start. To Howe, power had always been of more importance than place. Unfortunately, there was very little happening in Nova Scotia in that period to call forth his special talents.

Seated in his red plush chair on the government side of the House, he tried not to show his weariness and boredom. He wished passionately that he could get out of local politics for good. Yet in what other place could he be as useful? Here he was approaching sixty – still ambitious, still capable of high endeavour – yet even Johnny Russell, who knew him best, kept putting him off when he asked for an Imperial appointment. Why? He had his faults. None knew them better than he. One was lack of moderation. He would put up with abuse and injury for too long, then retaliate with more force than was necessary, as in the struggle with Lord Falkland. It made him enemies, but it seemed to be something he couldn't help. He fought as he worked, with all his heart and mind, using every weapon in reach, never stopping to calculate the benefit or disadvantage to himself. Blows delivered and received in the heat of battle were soon forgotten by him, but not always by his opponents.

He suspected that in certain quarters of London his outspokenness, even his integrity, were hated and feared. Perhaps he ought to have flattered and bribed his way to prizes as others had, but money and prestige were not the prizes he was after. He would be happy, for example, to go anywhere in the world, do anything honourable just for his expenses, if it was something which would further his dream of a united empire. Was his sense of mission, his long and varied experience in colonial affairs to be wasted, because there was no plan by which colonials could be drawn into the British public service? "Here is work for the highest intellects," he had pleaded with Russell, then Prime Minister, "for the purest patriotism on both sides of the Atlantic." But England, busy with foreign intrigues, had no time for the visions of a distant colonial. She continued to award her good positions and high honours to the voting inhabitants of two small islands.

Joe had for some time stopped listening to the dull speech of a dull speaker. Glancing with curiosity around the Assembly, he saw that the new men on both sides were all considerably younger than himself, shrewd, unsentimental sorts like Charles Tupper and Jonathon McCully and Adams Archibald. So many old faces missing. Huntington was gone. So was dear old Grigor. It was not always death that had taken his friends. That great humorist, Tom Haliburton, finding "radical" Nova Scotia uncongenial to his Tory taste, had departed for England, where, however, his home was always open to "that rascally Reformer, Howe" who had long ago forgiven his friend. Doyle, widowed, retired and ill, had gone to live with a sister in New York. Only Annand of the old Club was left, and Annand wasn't Annand any more.

Or perhaps he himself had changed. Was it a sign of advancing years that he believed all the really good fellows – men like Huntington, Bell, Uniacke and Doyle – were of former times? But they were the men who had helped win responsible government and he wished he had them with him now. Huntington, if he were alive, would have been the first to agree that Nova Scotia needed more than partial freedom; Uniacke, with his clear legal mind, would have contributed something of value to *The Organization of the Empire*, Howe's most recent explanation of the benefits to be enjoyed by all parts of a united empire; Doyle, if he were here, would quickly stir up this lacklustre House with his wit and mischief.

"I never went through a more laborious Session," he wrote Jane at the end of it. He had managed, however, to get another tentative agreement for an intercolonial railroad, and that summer he travelled to England to ask for concessions in support of it. While he was there, he received a summons from the Prime Minister's office.

He wrote the good news home in January. "My old friend, Lord Russell, has bestowed upon me in the most gracious manner the Commissionership of Fisheries." His task would be to oversee the final years of the Reciprocity Treaty with the United States as it related to the fisheries. It was not exactly what Joe would have chosen – he would have preferred something more challenging – but the pay was good and he had debts to pay. "It means I can get out of local politics at last, and for good," he rejoiced with Susan Ann. "No more campaigning in all sorts of weather, no more beating about the country, pushing and brow-beating party members, settling silly disputes and breaking up miserable intrigues." And when the treaty ended in a year or two, Lord Russell had promised to find something else for him, something better. Here at last was the first big step up the Imperial ladder to that position of importance in Britain!

He need not feel he was deserting his party, for he had taught them all he knew, and his lieutenant Adams Archibald had been trained by him to carry on the Liberal torch. Meanwhile, praise God, he was out of it all for good.

Had Joe the gift of the sight, as the Irish put it, he would have been shocked to learn that he had yet to fight some of the most vicious and vital election battles of his life.

CHAPTER SEVENTEEN
1863-1865

*"I resist the Quebec scheme of government because
I do not like it."*

Botheration Letter, 1865

"I am not, as you know, opposed in principle to union," Howe
told his friend Will Stairs in January 1863, "but why this sudden interest in it?" He had returned from his first voyage of
inspection around the cod ports to find Halifax highly excited
over the possibility of a confederation of the provinces. William
Stairs, a local hardware merchant and Member of the Assembly, frowned and shrugged.

"More than one reason," he said with a furrowed brow.
"Some nervous folk in New Brunswick and Canada are wondering what the Americans intend doing with all those unem-
ployed soldiers when their Civil War is over. Will they turn an
army loose on our borders? At the very least, Irish members
of that army might be transformed overnight into Fenian free-
booters." The Fenians were Irish agitators in the States who
threatened to invade the British colonies as a protest against
British rule in Ireland. "Our north-west is now opening to
settlement and the States might decide to take it over. You
know what they believe, that it's their manifest destiny to control the whole continent. Then Canada, with her huge debt and
her constant troubles with the French, sees union as her salva-
tion in both areas. As for us in the Maritimes, we could be
invaded by sea from Boston by the Americans *or* the Fenians."
Joe could see how these fears would work upon the minds of

the people in the British provinces, and could hear in his imagination the voices of Canadians like Cartier, McGee, Brown and Macdonald, for he had met them all and knew their views: "*We must unite, so the Americans will know that if they attack one, they must deal with all— As fragments we shall be lost— We must of course have representation by population— Mais non, parbleu!— What matters is that we have unity, no matter how!*"

"We cannot have union," said Joe Howe firmly, "until we have the intercolonial railway, if only for the passage of troops through British territory."

Stairs wondered aloud what Britain would have to say about it.

"Britain dreads trouble with the States." Joe ran his fingers through his hair, setting it wildly on end. "And of course the Little Englanders will be friends of union if it saves them a sixpence in tax to help maintain our defences. But I have a better answer to all these mournful cries," he said with vigour, "than a meagre six-province union in a country still half wilderness. With my organization of the Empire, the Queen would never need fear the States or any other combination of nations which could be formed against her."

After Stairs had left, Howe warned his wife to be careful what she said. "As a servant of the British government I am not supposed to take an active part in politics. And in this union business I'm just as pleased to stand aside. I shall cast my vote like any other citizen and let the majority decide."

With luck, he thought, the thing would die a natural death, like so many previous attempts to unite the Maritime provinces.

In March, Charles Tupper, Premier of Nova Scotia's Conservative government, moved in the House that delegates from Nova Scotia join those of New Brunswick and Prince Edward Island at Charlottetown, to again discuss a union of the three Maritime provinces. It would be a step, he admitted, towards a larger union later on. "It is not intended," he added, "to submit this question for the approval of the people, as ample opportunity has been afforded for its full and free discussion."

To Joe Howe the words were shocking. Not submit the

William Stairs (1789-1865) merchant, reformer, and anti-Confederate.

question to the people! Not allow them to vote on a change in their Constitution! Outraged not only in his sense of fair play but in his strongest political feelings, Joe no longer felt like a bystander. That this concerned only the small union made no difference. The right of the people to vote on what concerned them was why in the past thirty years he had fought not only the battle for responsible government but a dozen smaller ones. He went at once to see Adams Archibald, the man he had chosen to carry on the Liberal torch, the man who had seconded Tupper's motion.

"It has been our principle from the start," Joe reminded the younger man, "never to act on any matter of importance to the people without their expressed consent. To ignore that is to begin an erosion of the people's rights."

Archibald agreed. He had been well instructed over the years of their friendship. Still, he had never made any secret of his interest in union. "Strictly speaking," he said, his features controlled, emotionless as always, "that is true. Yet there is some truth in Tupper's claim that a cabinet is not expected to query the public on every issue."

"Sophistry!" snapped Howe. "This is no petty matter of a local by-law. It's a change in the Constitution. Why *not* appeal to the people? It's simple enough. Let both parties prepare a statement of how each stands on Maritime union and submit them to the public who, in the next election, will show by their votes which they want."

Archibald smiled faintly. "But if Tupper lost, could we be certain he lost for that reason, or because of his unpopular Education Bill last year? Besides," he went on before Joe could speak, "most men will vote by party on general issues, but this is something which cuts right across party lines. Look at the delegates – Tupper, Henry, Dickey for the Tories, myself and probably McCully for the Liberals. We're all working together for a change, for union."

Momentarily, the old warhorse in Joe stirred. But at once he reminded himself that he had to curb such instincts. He had made his move out of politics and must stick to it.

He did receive an invitation from Tupper to be one of the delegates, but since Lord Russell refused his request for leave, he had to turn the invitation down. He would like to have been at Charlottetown, to guard the interests of Nova Scotia and make sure she wasn't forced into Maritime union against her will. But, he told himself, this conference will probably fail too. They'd tried often enough before to join the three coastal provinces and had never even been able to agree on which provincial city should be the capital! By the time the larger union came to be considered, he would be finished with the fisheries and free to take a more active interest.

He left on the government steam corvette *Lily* a few days later to attend to his duties in the north, writing a cheerful letter to Jane on his first day at sea: "I have made a brisk exchange of a life of sedentary drudgery with 350,000 masters and £700 a year (half of which I had to give away or spend in elections to maintain my position) for a life in the open air and about £1,000, with ships to sail about in, new countries to see, and no master but the Queen."

In late October, the *Lily* put into St. John's Harbour, Newfoundland, and the first man Joe talked with ashore told him the news. The Charlottetown Conference had been invaded by George Brown, John A. Macdonald, George Cartier and others from Canada. The original purpose of the meeting had been shelved, in order to discuss a union of *all* the provinces. After that, things had moved at astonishing speed. At a meeting in Quebec a few weeks later, Seventy-Two Resolutions had been drawn up as a basis for union, and the delegates sent home to lay the Quebec Scheme, as it was called, before the public.

The news completely spoiled Joe's pleasure in the cruise.

On November 2, the *Lily* berthed at Halifax and Joe stepped ashore to find Halifax in a high state of excitement. Public meetings were to be held at once to hear the delegates' reports. Most of the local papers, including Annand's *Chronicle*, claimed Nova Scotia would welcome a confederation of all the provinces and that Joe Howe, for one, was warmly in favour. Joe read this with incredulity and shot off to the *Chronicle* office. There he discovered that Annand was away in England and the editor's chair was occupied by Jonathon McCully, one of the Union delegates to Charlottetown and Quebec. McCully, a big man with the rugged frame of a farmer and the no-nonsense look of his Ulster-Irish Presbyterian forbears, thrust out a belligerent jaw when Joe demanded to know what he was up to.

"You've said more than once that union must come."

"After the railway!"

"The intercolonial will be built, don't worry," said the other with satisfaction. "That was part of the bargain. From what you said at the dinner last summer, Howe, I was sure you'd come round altogether to union."

"Then you thought wrong." Joe recalled with vexation a convivial affair in honour of visiting Canadians. A public man, mellow with wine and food, should not be held accountable for everything he said in an after-dinner speech. "But even if I were for union in principle, I haven't yet laid eyes on this Quebec Scheme, so how could I be in favour of it?"

"I've printed no lies," said McCully doggedly.

"Something left out is just as false," Joe said with disgust. "You haven't said a word, I suppose, about my views on Imperial federation, though I've said a hundred times I'd prefer it to a union of the provinces."

"Oh I see what smarts, Howe," McCully grumbled. "This is Tupper's tune and you don't want to play second fiddle to the man who beat you in the last election."

"Oh for the lord's sake, McCully!" Joe slammed his fist on the desk in exasperation. Partisans like McCully could never separate politics from personalities. Joe Howe and Charles Tupper had fought each other all around the clock, in and out of the House for years, each playing as hard as he could for his own side. But when the game was over, you (figuratively speaking) shook hands. You couldn't spend your life brooding over political name-calling, or you might as well give up the game. Tupper understood this, if McCully didn't. "What puzzles me, is *your* change of heart. Only a few months ago, you were saying Canada would never regard us as equal partners, but only as a convenient makeweight to balance the French influence."

The other man shrugged. "That was before I knew they'd build the railroad."

Railroads. Of course. Railroads and politics went together like yoke and white in an egg. There were those who could see nothing but railroad charters and the fortunes to be made with them.

When he left the *Chronicle*, he assumed McCully would have the decency to stop writing about him, but he was wrong.

The paper proclaimed Howe a devoted Unionist right up to the moment Annand arrived home and fired McCully from the editorship, but by then the damage was done. It had cast Joe ahead of time in the role of a man who just didn't know his own mind. At Temperance Hall that evening, Joe met Adams Archibald before the meeting opened.

"The intercolonial railway will certainly be built," Archibald said, his face glowing with rare enthusiasm, "we insisted on that. Under one government, vast opportunities will open up." For ordinary men, wondered Joe, or just for politicians and railway contractors? For Nova Scotia, or only for Canada? And what about the man in the street, who was to have no say in how he was to be governed – by a group of backwoods Canadians or by the Queen of England and Parliament? "We are very lucky," continued Archibald, "to be in at the start."

"What is Nova Scotia asked to give in return for the railroad?"

"Well," the other paused. A methodical, painstaking man, Archibald had no doubt spent hours drawing up his report, weighing each word. He would find it hard to summarize. "I can tell you this much. I had a lot to do with the financial arrangements, and I made certain they were fair to Nova Scotia."

Before the speeches were a quarter over, Joe was grimly appalled. The Quebec Scheme fair to Nova Scotia? Tariff increases alone would be ruinous to the province.

When the meeting was over, men gathered eagerly around Joe Howe to see what he thought, but he refused to express any opinion at all. As a civil servant, he reminded them, he was expected to stay out of politics. He listened though to what they had to say.

Almost at once, he was reassured. There had been opposition in the country to Tupper's motion from the start – "It's something cooked up by those fellows in Halifax, looking for profit to themselves." Gradually in Halifax too, and without Joe's help, opposition began to grow. An Anti-Confederate League of city merchants, led by Will Stairs and Jerry Northup, was formed, and increasing numbers of country Members

177

came out strong against the Scheme, arguing that its adoption would lead to the loss of Nova Scotia's financial and political independence. Then came word that Tilley's pro-Union government in New Brunswick had fallen, and there was jubilation in the League. Prince Edward Island had shown no interest in the Quebec Scheme and Newfoundland hadn't been approached. If New Brunswick, lying fair across the road to Canada, should hold out against union, the whole bothering business would fall on its face.

The House was soon aware of the general feeling, and Tupper dared not introduce a union motion which might, if defeated, bring down his government. Even a dispatch from London putting the colonial office's seal of approval on the Quebec Scheme, did not cause many to change their minds. It did not disturb Joe Howe, who was sure the Mother Country would never try to force union through against the people's wishes. He did write a series of letters anonymously for the *Chronicle*, commenting unfavourably on the Scheme. He wrote in his usual style and everyone guessed the author, but by the time the *Botheration Letters*, as they were called, appeared in print, the first enthusiasm in Nova Scotia for union had died anyway.

Joe went off in June of 1865 to his duties with an easier mind. These duties now took him south to Washington and New York, where he was expected to tidy up the department's affairs in preparation for the ending of the Treaty. He was also scheduled to appear as the Nova Scotian delegate at a convention in Detroit in July to discuss the possibility of a new trade treaty.

The Civil War had just ended and Joe, curious as always, visited many of the battlefields while at the same time trying to get word of his son Frederick, who had joined the Northern Army as an officer in the Ohio Regiment. "Returning late on Saturday from a long walk," he wrote his younger son, Will, in the course of a letter running to some twenty pages, "I met an Ohio soldier who told me headquarters had arrived and were just down the street. I increased my pace and, finding some horses around my hotel door, went in and astonished Fred who was sitting among his companions resting after a long

day's ride. He got leave of absence, and we spent that afternoon and night and Sunday night together for which great
mercy, after all he has gone through, I fervently thank God."
He gave a proud account of Fred's adventures in several
famous battles and listed his excellent commendations.

Then it was time to go to Detroit, where five hundred of the
leading statesmen and businessmen of the United States made
it very clear to the fifty British delegates that they did not
intend to renew the Reciprocity Treaty or make a new one.
The outnumbered British tried for two days to change their
minds, without success. Joe's contribution was to come on the
third and final day.

"The room was hot," he said afterwards, "and the speeches
long drawn out. I was physically tired and began to feel a foreboding that I would not be equal to the occasion." Excusing
himself, he left the hall and walked along the street until he
came to a bar-room and went in. He found workingmen taking
their beer and joined them, got them interested in his stories
and soon lifted himself out of his depressed mood. In fact, he
forgot time altogether until suddenly the doors burst open and
two members of the British delegation, spotting him, shouted –
"Howe! We've been looking everywhere for you. It's time for
your speech!"

They bundled him off in a hurry, to the vast disappointment
of his drinking companions and minutes later, in his place on
the platform, Joe was briefly introduced.

"I never prayed for the gift of eloquence until now," he
began. He stood there before that huge audience – an ordinary
looking man of past sixty, with a large white face and somewhat shaggy eyebrows under a massive forehead. He was personally known to only a few, and his face wore a diffident
smile. He paused to cast a considering eye around the room.
Then, taking a deep breath, and shrugging his coat back on his
shoulders in a way Nova Scotians would instantly have recognized, he began to give the speech of his life.

By the end of it, he had them laughing and crying, tossing
their hats in the air, shouting and waving handkerchiefs, and
when the excitement had partially subsided, an American

delegate jumped up and moved the Treaty be renewed. The motion was promptly seconded and unanimously carried.

When he got home, Susan Ann held out to him an official-looking envelope; it was a summons from the Prime Minister of England to go overseas immediately. Joe thought for a moment, then laughed. "They've had time to hear about the Detroit speech and they want to compliment me in person." He was only half-joking. What else could they want him for? "A governor will be needed soon for British Columbia," he remarked and saw hope spring to his wife's eyes. "I wouldn't mind going out there to show what I could do." He sailed for England nearly sure that Britain had a new job for him, quite possibly the governorship of her newest North American colony.

He was received at 10 Downing Street by Johnny Russell, now Earl Russell and for the second time Prime Minister of England. After a warm handshake and several highly complimentary remarks on the Detroit triumph, the Prime Minister paused for a moment, then said with apparent casualness: "The proposal to unite the British provinces is causing some excitement in Nova Scotia, I hear."

"It is, sir."

"There is disagreement?"

"Not only in Nova Scotia."

"You are not opposed to it?" the other man persisted and Joe felt a sharp pang of disappointment. Not British Columbia. Something to do with union.

"I'm afraid I am, sir, but as a British government servant, my opinion counts for little."

"Nonsense," Russell said with sudden bluntness. "We both know that in or out of government, your voice is the voice of Nova Scotia's majority. If you won't support union, Howe, will you give me your word not to put obstacles in its way?"

So that was it. This was why he had been brought across the ocean. The Prime Minister had not been surprised that he was opposed. He'd been warned, by Tupper, probably, and now asked for a promise that he would mind his own business, let

180

union come, as Britain wanted. It would be simple to agree. In return, when a new appointment opened up, Howe would be the one to get it. Perhaps one was already open. A bribe was being offered.

The silence seemed long, but probably lasted only seconds, before he answered the Prime Minister.

"I regret, sir, that I can give no promise. I do not like this Quebec Scheme."

The Prime Minister made no reference to Imperial appointments but simply argued for two hours or more, trying to change Howe's mind. When asked what he had, in the main, against union, Joe told him: "Representation by population would mean we'd be forever swamped by the upper provinces. The plan of double legislatures couldn't be put in force without raising our duties immediately from 10 to 20 per cent. But there is another reason which, in my opinion, is the vital one. In England, no important change in the machinery of government is ever made without an appeal to the country. In the United States, no amendment can be made to the Constitution which is not approved by two-thirds of the Members of both Houses and ratified by the voters. You will therefore readily understand how we would feel if our institutions, enjoyed for a century, were swept away without our approval." He added that he hoped the British government would not stain itself by helping or approving the movement towards Confederation. He said he would write out the rest of his objections and submit a paper. While he was about it, he added, he would do one on his plan for *Imperial* federation. The paper would be called "Organization of the Empire."

CHAPTER EIGHTEEN
1865-1866

"I, for the first time in my life, hesitate between duty and interest."

Letter to Susan Ann, March 1866

"It is evident," Joe wrote his wife the night after his interview with Russell, "they are very anxious to get my support to the measure, but I did not disguise my opinions and made a holy show of it before we were done." He told her she was not to worry. He had faith in his own powers and was accustomed to trust to Providence. He was sure if he worked hard and demonstrated to England that Imperial federation was a better solution than provincial confederation, all would be well.

Before leaving England, Joe was saddened to receive word of Jane's death, though it was not unexpected. She was in her seventies and had been ill. "I had no desire that she should linger," he wrote Jane's daughter Sarah, "and was rather rejoiced when I learnt that the scene had closed." He added with wry humour – "I am not exactly 'the last Rose of Summer left blooming alone' but the last stem of a somewhat stately growth left standing amidst the mould of all the others." Then, shaking off gloom and sadness, he went on to describe "a most delightful summer abounding in novelty, interest and instruction." In accordance with his beloved sister's advice, he was still casting about everywhere for knowledge and experience.

The year 1866 began quietly enough with his departure for the States again, his mind easier in spite of the colonial office attitude. England might still hope for union, but in Nova

Scotia, even in the legislature, discussion and argument had nearly died.

His worries were now the familiar ones, finding a job and paying his debts. The Americans had not followed up their resolution at Detroit and when the Treaty ended in March, Joe would be out of work. He still had some family to support. His oldest son, Joe, was a merchant seaman sailing at the moment in the Indian Ocean and Fred had settled down in the States after the war; Ellen was married and living in Montreal. Will was still too young to be employed, however, and Syd, who had left the navy due to ill health was still without a steady position. Edward had died, leaving a wife and several small children. A large salary would not be necessary. He could probably earn all he needed at literary work, something he had always wanted to do anyway. "Poetry was my first love, politics the harridan I married!" He prepared himself for his new career with his usual energy.

In Washington after his regular work for the Fisheries Department was done, he wrote articles and essays for the American papers on political subjects. He enjoyed the actual writing but the monetary returns were less than he'd hoped. Could he support his family and pay his debts on such meagre pay? Then came the miracle.

"My dear Susan Ann," he wrote jubilantly from New York on January 15, 1866, "Providence seems to provide for us, often in modes very unexpected and often at just the right time. I had hardly arrived here when an application was made to me by Mr. William B. Morrell, who has purchased the *New York Albion*, to edit that paper after the 31st of March next. The offer was made in the most flattering terms, it being assumed that the views and policy of the speech at Detroit would guide my pen in the conduct of the paper. He will pay me thirty-five hundred dollars to edit the *Albion*, adding another five hundred if it prospers. This astonished me very much, as it will you. Here at all events is our bread and cheese, a living for my family and an honourable and influential position independent of local politics or of friends over the sea. For this new and unexpected mercy, I fervently thank God. It makes me feel more independent of all chances and casualties than I have done for many a day."

Meanwhile, no longer having an expense account, he had to keep down his cost of living. "I have moved to lodgings where I pay ten dollars a week and find my own fires," he wrote Susan Ann, "burning wood which costs about two dollars a week. I breakfast and dine at a restaurant for a dollar sixty-five. Newspapers and street-cars cost about thirty-five cents more. A bottle of sherry and another of whisky costs a dollar-fifty each, so I have something to offer whoever comes in, and get off cheap for drinking. I read and write every forenoon, then go down and hear the debates."

He was happy and free at last from worry and responsibility. He pictured Susan Ann and himself spending a few years in New York, living a life of infinite variety and freedom in the company of the Doyles and a dozen other friends. Then, with all their bills paid and a little something put by for the future, they could return to finish out a comfortable old age in Nova Scotia. This rosy dream faded with the arrival of letters from Halifax hinting at trouble. Annand's paper, said the Halifax correspondent, had suggested a *conference to discuss union on terms other than the Quebec Scheme*. Now why had he done so when all the furor was nearly over? Was it a move to please Britain, or was Annand looking for a chance to get out and join what might become the winning side? Joe thought that un-likely. It was probably one of Will's devious manoeuvres to delay the Opposition until the Session closed.

Another letter was from Annand himself, fretting because Sir Fenwick Williams, the new Governor, had said nothing about union in his Speech from the Throne. It wasn't natural! The governors of the other provinces had featured it in their speeches, so why not Sir Fenwick? "Is something going on in the background that we don't know about?"

A merchant friend sent a note and a news item. The news item was clipped from a Canadian paper and reported a speech of John A. Macdonald's in which the Conservative leader said union was certain to pass in a few weeks. "Something's up, Howe. Can you come home? We need your leadership badly.

Of course nothing should be allowed to interfere with any plans you have made for your future, but if you were not otherwise engaged we would see you were not out of pocket." Oh no, thought Joe, no more! No more living on hand-outs from Members who were busy attending to their private careers and had no time for politics. Many of the men who had started out with him had piled up fortunes in the intervening years and now they expected him to give up the first real security he had ever had to come home and once again pull the chestnuts out of the fire. No. This time Nova Scotia must find another man to work for her. Tupper, he thought involuntarily, must be in something of a sweat if he hoped to push a union motion through this Session. Only four weeks of it left, and nothing definite yet from New Brunswick.

At home in Halifax, Susan Ann was growing anxious. She was hearing all sorts of rumours and was aware of the mounting excitement. She knew too that Joseph's anti-Confederate friends were begging for his return, and she prayed he would hold out against them.

On March 14, Howe received a letter from Morrell enclosing his contract for the editorship. All it needed was his signature.

He kept receiving messages from Halifax – a by-election in New Brunswick showed union feeling there much stronger. The militia of Canada had been called out to meet any possible Fenian uprising on St. Patrick's Day, something which would have an effect on waverers in Nova Scotia. In spite of everything, he felt an urgency to be on the spot, to see and hear for himself what was going on. He crushed the feeling down. Plenty of anti-Confederates in the House. It was up to them to stop any move on Tupper's part. Nothing could go wrong so long as the Members held fast. Still . . .

He sat for a long time gazing blindly at the wall in front of him, picturing scenes in Halifax and throughout the province, trying to convince himself he was no longer needed. Going back would mean giving up the *Albion*. He could not expect Morrell to hold the job open indefinitely. It would mean plunging again into the great dirty mud puddle of politics. No! Out of the question!

With a sigh, he took paper and pen and began a letter to Susan Ann, explaining his fears and doubts. "I am pressed by Morrell to go to New York and accept the chair on the 31st. I am much inclined to accept, half inclined to throw up everything, come home and fight the battle of my own country in the dark hours that I see are closing around her. That would be the right thing to do. But we have had so much thankless care and labour that I, for the first time in my life, hesitate between duty and interest. Poor old Nova Scotia. God help her. Beset with marauders outside and enemies within, she has a hard time of it – and my mouth closed and my pen silent. Write to me when you can, but do not expect long letters. I am lonely – weary – vexed."

He wrote this on March 12. On March 20, he heard from an anti-Confederate that Miller talked of backing Annand's suggestion for a new conference. Miller, the very vocal anti-Union Member for Richmond, was a man who boasted that he recognized no leader but always acted with perfect independence. He was a persuasive speaker who had served the anti-Confederates well, but was not much liked by his colleagues. "There is certainly a definite movement in the direction of union," the letter went on. "I think some of our people are being bought. If they're making a deal, Joe, it's all up with us. Can't you come?"

Joe crumpled the letter in his hand. They must understand, once and for all, no matter what the urgency, he could no longer help. The *Albion* contract lay on his table. He snatched it, signed in the space provided, and blotted it with a firm hand. He then went out and sent a telegram to Jerry Northup, who would be sure to spread the word: "*A free man. Have accepted Morrell's offer.*"

The following day a letter arrived from Annand. "Sir Fenwick Williams suggests that I propose on the floor of the House that a new conference be held in London under the auspices of the colonial office, to work out the details of a new plan of union."

Joe stared at the words, stunned. A *new* conference. To be held in *London*! Under the auspices of the *colonial office*! England was going to use every means in her power, short of force, to make the Maritime legislatures accept Confederation!

"I asked time to consider," Annand's letter continued, and Joe breathed again. Thank God, Will had dithered as usual. But, thought Joe with fresh dismay, even if Annand refused to play Tupper's game, there might be others who would, if the rewards were high enough.

Once again he was torn, pulled first toward that pleasant anxiety-free life he and his wife had so well and truly earned, then toward Nova Scotia, the beloved country whose people were having their rights swept away by Tupper and the Canadians. Members of the Assembly alone stood in the way of Tupper's path, and if it was true they were thinking only of what prizes they might win by compliance with Canada, then who was thinking of Nova Scotia?

Joe picked up the *Albion* contract and tore it across and across. Seven days later, on March 27, 1866 he was back in Halifax prepared for battle.

CHAPTER NINETEEN
1866-1869

*"I am labouring to keep our people within the bounds
of loyalty and discretion."*

Letter to Macdonald, 1868

As his ship dropped anchor, Howe saw the changes that had
taken place in his short absence. There were military tents on
George's Island and guns at target practice on McNab's. In the
town he met worried groups talking and speculating. Seeing
him, they hurried to speak to him. "Howe!" They shook
hands and asked eagerly "What do you think? Can we depend
on Britain's aid if we go against her wishes? What about the
Irish? Have you heard any news?"

He reassured them, said he thought the Fenian danger exag-
gerated. It might even have been deliberate. The Fenian Scare
could not have been better timed for Tupper and Macdonald.
Joe went to see Annand next, and that uneasy Member was
only too thankful to hand over the reins.

"No more intrigues," Joe warned him. "No more talk of
conferences."

His next visit was to Adams Archibald to try to induce him
to abandon his partnership with Tupper. "The appeals were
splendid," said one man who was present at the meeting,
"pierced through and through with all the earnestness of Mr.
Howe's nature. Archibald listened – I will not say unmoved, for
he was deeply moved – but with deference, to the man whom
he had followed from his youth and to whom he had used to

188

look up as his ideal. He listened but yielded not."

"The people," he said, "through their representatives will decide."

"A few," countered his old leader, "will decide a matter which will affect all. Parliament has not the power to make so important a change without first appealing to the people."

It was McCully who spoke then, with a kind of brutal carelessness: "Parliament has the power to do anything but change a man into a woman."

Joe turned on him. "And you, McCully, may have the power to knock out your mother's brains, but the act if done will still be murder."

"As long as the majority of the Legislature stand firm," Joe warned his supporters in the House, "Tupper can do nothing."

The Parliament of Nova Scotia opened and there was no mention of union for three days. Then, on April 3, the anti-Confederate, William Miller, rose and asked a question which grew into a long and eloquent speech in which he said he was still opposed to the Quebec Scheme, but would be willing to favour a new conference in Britain, leaving the details to the arbitration of the Imperial Government, properly advised by delegates from all the provinces. Annand had grown very red in the face by the time Miller finished, for Miller's motion was in essence what the Governor had asked him, Annand, to introduce. Miller had got in first, by the back door so to speak, and would receive the reward, in case there should be any. Samuel MacDonell, the Member from Inverness, rose next and made a shorter, rather more awkward, speech in support. In the battle against union, Nova Scotia's first line of defence began to crumble.

Years later, MacDonell confided to a friend that Miller had made him believe Annand and other "anti's" were negotiating with the other side, planning to accept Confederation. "We had better get into line," Miller is supposed to have said, "anticipate Annand ... or we shall be left out in the cold and lose all chance of obtaining any of the good positions." Whether or not all or part of this was true, one fact is undeniable – William Miller and Samuel MacDonell were two of the Senators appointed to the first Dominion Government.

Joe strove to keep his troops cheerful. "There's still plenty of firmness in the House," he said. But Miller's speech had broken the dam. Tupper, taken by surprise by the speech – or so he said – lost no time introducing a resolution along the lines Miller had suggested. The deluge followed. One after the other, Members fell and the resolution for a new conference passed.

"Very well," said Joe Howe. "Now we must find out how the people feel!"

He toured the province making speeches and listening to opinions. "We couldn't find five hundred Confederates from Windsor to Yarmouth," he wrote Susan Ann. "As I go on, I feel more and more that I am in the path of duty and so far my voice has stood the strain." He was, in fact, striking right and left in his old style. Never did his enemies try harder to put him down. They said he had always been a Unionist and had reversed himself to get office, that he was jealous of Tupper and was out for revenge, and that he was going to ruin Nova Scotia by his stand against Confederation.

But the people of Nova Scotia said, "Go to England, Howe, and tell them we don't want it."

So that summer, with Will Annand and Hugh McDonald, Joe went off to England. They fought for months with every weapon they could use against the combined forces of Tupper, the Canadians, Britain's Parliament, and most of the press of England and Canada. The victory went, as it generally does, to the stronger side. On March 29, 1867, the Queen gave her assent to the passing of the British North America Act, thus creating a Dominion to be known as Canada, to extend from the Atlantic to the Pacific – and to include Nova Scotia, whether she liked it or not.

"The debates would not have done credit to a college union," Joe wrote home with bitter outrage. "If disloyal men can be made at all, it is by such treatment."

He was convinced that the Members of both British Houses, those few who had shown up for the debates, had made up their minds beforehand that the provinces were a source of peril and expense. "The prevailing idea is to set us adrift," he wrote Stairs, "to gradually withdraw British troops and to have no quarrel with the United States on account of us. There is to be a boat race on the Thames tomorrow, between the young fellows of Cambridge and Oxford. It creates more excitement than would be occasioned if British America were sunk in the sea."

To Susan Ann he wrote more cheerfully: "As you may suppose, the last fortnight has been one of anxiety and vexation, but do not fret about my disappointment. I never could have been happy had I not fought the battle through, and when it is over will face the future with a light heart." For, in his view, the battle was not over.

First, those who had tricked Nova Scotia into union must be punished. If every Member could be defeated in the coming elections, Britain must see that the delegates had lied when they said Nova Scotia was willing to join Confederation. Then it might be possible to have the British North America Act repealed. If the appeal were refused, they would ask to have the Act revised.

Before he left England, Joe received a letter from Will Stairs, assuring him that all the members of the Anti-Confederate League were grateful for what he had tried to do. They were aware of his low financial state and would understand if he stopped any line of public action which might mean further sacrifices. He was free, in other words, to step down and nobody would blame him. On the other hand, Stairs admitted, if he chose to run in the coming elections and would go to Ottawa afterwards as an independent Member, his aid would be of the greatest value to Nova Scotia when the new federal government got down to business.

Joe replied that he had thought long and had come to the conclusion that "perplexed and comparatively defenceless as our people must be for some time, I am hardly at liberty to desert them now at the very crisis of their affairs and when some guidance may be required." He also wrote, apologetically, to his wife: "The battle must be fought out before I can think of my own interests, or yours either."

The first Dominion Day celebration was a bitter one for most Nova Scotians. Flags hung at half-mast and all the anti-Confederate newspapers came out with their pages bordered in black. Then, with July First behind them, the Punishment Party set out to wipe the Confederates off the map. "Under Confederation," Joe's Repeal Party cried, "we will be a dependency of the cursed Canadians!"

The Union Party retorted with words like "progress" and "future prosperity." "The possession of coal mines," Tupper's paper declared, "together with other natural advantages, must in the course of time make Nova Scotia the great emporium for manufactures in British America."

"Progress!" snorted the *Novascotian* and *Chronicle*, "We *have* been rich – our ships *have* whitened the oceans of the world, and our people *have* prospered in lumbering and ship-building. Now all this will disappear."

"Disunited," insisted the Union press, "we were petty and insignificant. United we have the makings of a nation."

"A nation," said Howe with scorn, "in which all our money is swept away to dig canals or fortify Montreal."

"This union," claimed Adams Archibald, "will not only open up a wider field for public men, it will soften the asperities of political life."

"It will take the wisdom of Solomon," Joe contradicted, "and the energy and strategy of Frederick the Great to weld a people with so few cohesive qualities into a new nationality. Ever since the union of Upper and Lower Canada, the French Canadians by sticking together have controlled the legislation and the government. They will do the same thing in a larger union and, as the English will split and divide as they always do, the French Members will in nine cases out of ten be masters of the situation. But should a chance combination thwart them, then they will back their local Legislature against the united Parliament and in less than five years will as assuredly separate from the confederacy as Belgium did from Holland."

As election time drew near, Adams Archibald was offered the office of Secretary of State for the Provinces. To take possession of it he needed the approval of the people. He therefore made an impressive effort to capture their votes, driving through the country with a brass band and arriving at Truro with more than a hundred carriages and wagons full of supporters. A reporter present could not recall the order of the speeches, but thought Dr. Tupper led off with Mr. Howe following.

"Mr. Howe began by describing the long and close friendship that had existed between himself and Archibald. 'I watched the career of my son in the Liberal faith,' he said, 'each year more fully persuaded that, whatever might happen to me, the Liberal Party would have a shining light to lead them in their bright and in their gloomy periods. But what did I see?' The fire, the pathos, the sorrow that moved him to tears, the ring of voice with which he denounced Archibald for selling his countrymen for the price of a sheepskin, the trip-hammer-like repetition of the words 'the man I trusted' and 'decent regard for the people' uttered with a solemnity like that of a tolling bell, all combined to make the occasion a very impressive one. It was as if Howe were pronouncing a death sentence upon his own son."

Archibald had to follow this speech and was unable to shake off the hypnotic influence of his old leader. From that hour, his defeat was certain.

His was not the only defeat. Almost the whole of the Union Party was wiped out in the Dominion election. Tupper alone survived. In the provincial one, held at the same time, only two Confederates were returned. There was no doubt how Nova Scotia stood on Confederation. The Punishment Party had been a success.

"And now what do we do?" the Repealers asked Howe, "refuse to attend the Federal Parliament – or go, and therefore seem to acknowledge Confederation as an accepted fact?"

"We will go under protest," said Howe, "refuse to connect

193

ourselves with either Canadian party, neither ask nor accept favours, and make it clear we intend to ask Britain for Repeal."

Joe wrote Susan Ann from Ottawa that, on his arrival, he was surprised and touched to have old Canadian and New Brunswick friends greet him without rancour and new ones beg to make his acquaintance. "All I would have to do at this point is say 'Oh well, after all, I suppose we must submit and make the best of it' and I could then make my way fast enough to the honours and profits of the Dominion. But, thankful for all God's mercies, we will keep on in the path of duty."

As usual, interested in everything, he enjoyed his stay in Ottawa and was a great success in the legislative debates. "Thursday I spoke for an hour in opposition to the proposal for purchasing the Hudson Bay territory and was heard by the whole House with unflagging interest. Last night I spoke for two hours, reviewing the whole course of the debate and paying off some fellows who had taken liberties with me. I kept the whole House laughing and have been much complimented on both speeches."

Shortly after this triumph, the Session over, he was back in Halifax.

At a crowded meeting in Halifax called to appoint a delegation to England to ask for repeal, Howe warned that such an appeal could be fruitless. There were sounds of dismay.

"What do we do then to show the Queen we mean business?" someone asked belligerently.

"Keep the peace," he answered at once. "Until your appeal is answered, maintain order as you always have."

"And if the answer's 'no'?"

"Aye, what then," another voice shouted. Before Joe could reply, an angry shout came from the back of the hall: "I know what I intend to do, take my gun and shoot the first Canadian who crosses our border!"

Joe's heart chilled as other voices echoed the speaker's. To his dismay, he thought he recognized one or two as those of House Members. Glancing around the room, reading the faces, he made a rapid estimate of the effect the words were having on this emotional audience. The gush of heated language must be stopped.

"One moment!" He pointed a wrathful finger at the man who had first spoken. "There's one thing I do know. There is no greater peril any party can run than that of being misled by hasty, ill-judging leaders."

The cries fell to a sullen mutter, in which Joe heard the word "annexation" several times. He ignored it and, with his speaker's skill, gradually brought the crowd around to reason and good humour. They asked him in the end to lead a delegation to London to ask for the repeal of the British North America Act. Though with small desire for another long trial of strength in Britain, Joe agreed to go.

This time he was able to take Susan Ann with him, no doubt at the expense of the Repeal Party. She kept a diary during those months in Britain, one of the few writings of hers that have survived, and in it she gives a careful account of their activities, even the entertainments they found time for – "At the Hippodrome this evening, we saw a three-year-old boy perform very wonderfully on the high bar ... We went afterward to a rather fast place, not frequented much by ladies, but with Joseph I can go everywhere. I did not notice any improprieties."

By the time Annand and two other Repealers arrived, Joe's eyes were giving him trouble. Susan Ann had to read the papers to him and do most of his copying. In an age without typewriters – the first was invented that year – all had to be written out by hand, and copies made the same way. It was not a holiday Nova Scotia had sent them on. It was, in fact, a heartbreaking business trying to catch the attention of even a few of London's busy citizens, most of whom had never even heard of Nova Scotia.

Returning to their lodgings one evening, they found Dr. Tupper had called and left his card. "We were honoured by a visit from Tupper," Joe reported to Will Stairs in a letter home, "though he never called last year. I returned the visit four or five days after, and had an hour's talk with him."

The talk, as often happens, was reported differently by each

party. Tupper wrote Sir John A. that he had told Howe he would
not attempt to stop his appeal but only try, when the Repealers
were beaten, to influence his future course. He had offered his
help, he said, if Howe would agree to enter the Dominion
Cabinet and work to strengthen Canada. "Together," he said
he told Howe, "we can rally the support of three-quarters of
the wealth, education and influence of the province." Joe, having just demonstrated in the election that he already had 90 per
cent, must have smiled. "Of course," he wrote home, "he
assumes we will be beaten here and is most anxious about
what is to come after. He is desirous that we shall then lay
down our arms. He thinks the Canadians will offer us any
terms and that he and I might rule the Dominion."

"He appeared deeply impressed," Tupper wrote Macdonald.

"I gave him no satisfaction," wrote Joe, "but chaffed him
all around the compass, and frightened him occasionally."

On May 20, Mrs. Howe wrote in her journal that Mr. Bright
had told the delegates it would be hopeless to ask for repeal
outright. It might be difficult even to get the promise of a parliamentary inquiry. John Bright, a Quaker M.P. who believed in
shaping public opinion before making an appeal to Parliament,
a fairly new idea then, had been chosen as the Nova Scotians'
spokesman in the Commons. Howe knew he was their best
hope, but most fervently he wished he could stand up there in
the House of Commons himself and sway the British ministers
as he had swayed the people of Southampton and Detroit!

Dr. Tupper's appearances in Hanover Street, where the
Howes lodged, seemed to bother Annand. He said he had it on
good authority that Tupper had been seen talking with Mr.
Bright too.

"So?" Joe asked impatiently. He had a mail to catch and,
disturbed at his writing, found it hard to control his annoyance
with Annand, who of late had become a nagging and fretful
colleague.

"Bright's *our* man!"

"He's his *own* man. Nobody can influence him against his
convictions, and he believes in our cause. That's why we chose
him."

"But why does Tupper always talk to you privately?"

"Why don't you ask him!" Annand gave up then, but a few days later came rushing in, his face red and furious.

"Tupper is telling everyone that if the British Parliament refuses our petition, we'll quietly accept Confederation." He looked accusingly at Joe. "Did you say that?"

"On the contrary." Joe rubbed tired eyes. "I said Nova Scotia would never be satisfied until she was treated with respect and justice. Go after the members of Britain's Parliament, Will, not Tupper. They're the men we have to worry about."

On June 16, Susan Ann's diary reads: "Joseph, Annand, Smith, Troop, Northup and Garvie went to the House of Commons this evening to hear Mr. Bright present the petition and speak, which he did well. But the British government had already decided against us, and have handed us over to the mercy of the Canadians. We must be patient and see what comes next. I pray it may not lead to bloodshed."

Before a House only half filled, Mr. Bright had fought with all the oratory and argument at his command, using Joe's notes to guide him. He got only eighty-seven votes in favour of an inquiry, and two hundred and thirteen voted against even this compromise. The only concession was to appoint the Duke of Buckingham to study the British North America Act in order to see what could be done to make it less financially oppressive to Nova Scotia. The Duke promptly passed this chore over to the Canadians.

Joe Howe walked out of the British House of Commons that night with the passionate determination never to go there on such an errand again. He felt a sense of humiliation not easy to describe. Even his old friend Russell had voted nay. Needing to be alone, he asked the others to meet him later at the Howe lodgings in Hanover Square, and walked down through crowds of uncaring Londoners to Victoria Embankment.

Standing there beside the Thames, he felt the sickness of defeat mix with the anger always excited in him by injustice. Tasting this bitter mixture, he imagined himself giving the order for revolt, actually saw himself in his mind's eye lead an army of Nova Scotians with bands playing, banners flying, muskets pointed at Montreal and Toronto! It was only for a moment that the vision lasted and then, in spite of his misery, he had to smile at the ludicrous picture. Oh they might make some show against the Canadians for a short time, but what would Britain be doing meanwhile? A flagship in Halifax Harbour would be raking the waterfront with her guns, a British garrison in the Citadel pouring shot down the hill into the streets. As for the province, Britain's navy could have a gunboat in every one of her open harbours in less than ten days.

In a cooler frame of mind, he thought of Nova Scotia's fruitful orchards, her fields and farms, her fishing coves and busy harbours, and saw them ravaged by civil war. He pictured her men, women and children, most of them known to him personally, falling wounded or dead. Then, in one of his "flashes" he saw what a frightening responsibility was his, and what he had to do. If he, of all men, could envision revolution, others less loyal and devoted could do the same. Men like those who had shouted at the meeting for Repeal, for instance, would not hesitate for a minute if he sent out a call to arms. This must never happen. Any fool could plunge a country into war, and there were fools everywhere; but to make those at home see they must accept the situation, no matter how hard, and keep the peace – this was the job before him.

The matter was urgent too for Nova Scotians everywhere would be waiting to hear how their champions in England had made out. What if, when they heard, they gave way to despair and allowed themselves to be led by a few hotheads into revolt or annexation? Just one spark could set the whole province on fire. He and his fellow delegates must make sure that such a spark was not struck. Their immediate task then would be to write a dispatch to the Nova Scotia government warning them to keep the populace calm and reassured until they could hear the whole story from the delegates in person.

On the ship going home, he and his colleagues could lay the groundwork for negotiations. Tupper would be on the same ship, and they would feel out his intentions and those of his Canadian colleagues, at the same time letting him know what

Nova Scotia expected in the way of better terms. Better terms, that was the goal now! Nova Scotia must not come out of this defeat empty-handed!

With a somewhat lighter heart, Joe turned his steps toward Hanover Square. As he hurried through the park, it crossed his mind with another bitter pang, that a Mother Country, who cared so little for the concerns of one of her most loyal colonies, was unlikely ever to listen to Joe Howe's plan for drawing tighter the bonds of Empire. Even John Bright had called such a federation a dream. The times were not right for his inspiration, Joe sadly conceded. Perhaps when the day of the Little Englanders had passed, perhaps long after he himself was dead, Great Britain might wake to the importance of consolidating the Empire in some sort of co-operative commonwealth. Meanwhile, Joe Howe had other work at hand.

The delegates returned to Nova Scotia prepared to deal with the Canadians and in apparent agreement that there would be no talk of revolt or annexation. It was therefore a shock when Annand told Howe that his government – he was Premier – intended to make one last appeal to Britain.

"But in London you agreed with us," Joe exclaimed. "What changed your mind?"

"I think we may have better luck after a change of ministry in England, particularly if we can induce New Brunswick and Prince Edward Island to join in the appeal. Perhaps we didn't do all we might have done this time," said Annand.

Joe stared at him in disbelief, thinking of the endless struggle overseas to make their cause heard. But then, come to think of it, Annand hadn't always been there. He'd been away on business of his own quite often.

"Very well," he said slowly, "if the Nova Scotia government decides to make another appeal, it must take place; but while you're sending out resolutions and appeals, the rest of us will test the sincerity of the Canadians." He reminded Annand of the fact that Macdonald and other leading Canadians were coming to Halifax next month to hear Nova Scotia's complaints. "Some sort of convention of all those opposed to Confederation ought to meet before their arrival to decide what we will say to them."

Annand agreed to call such a convention and it opened in the Assembly chamber one morning shortly after. On the very first day, Joe saw that it had been a mistake. He was appalled to hear suggestions for open resistance to the law and plans to insult the visiting Canadians. Someone, too, mentioned an incomprehensible plot to seize the provincial revenues before the Canadians could lay hands on it. For a while he said nothing, just listened, but at last he rose to his feet and the room fell instantly quiet.

Soberly, he asked the Members to turn their backs absolutely on such suggestions, which could lead only to death and destruction. "If life is to be lost and property wasted," he said, "those who favour such methods should take the lead. If the people respond to your call to arms, be prepared to lead them and history will record your martyrdom, if not your achievements." He waited a moment to see if anyone wished to move a resolution for independence, but no one did. "Very well," he said grimly, "there is one other thing you can do." All eyes turned to him. "Let all the Members of both Houses go up with the Cabinet at their head to the Governor and resign, saying you will not work for or under him as long as he holds a commission from Ottawa and not from the Queen. I pledge myself that if such a resolution is adopted, I and every Member of the House of Commons in Ottawa that I can influence, will back you – resign our seats and pile up such a majority as cannot be misrepresented in England." Once more he waited, scanning the faces, but not a man rose to second the motion and he knew then that the convention cared nothing for the country, but only for office. From that moment he took no part in repeal movements.

It was no surprise when Annand refused to meet the Canadians or when his two newspapers began a campaign of violent abuse against the Nova Scotian negotiators and the "Ottawa crowd."

In October, Sir John A. Macdonald wrote Howe that the

federal government was ready to discuss better terms – new financial arrangements, that is, which would make up for the income Nova Scotia would lose in taxes and trade because of Confederation. Sir John offered to put his finance minister, Sir John Rose, in touch with any gentlemen selected for the purpose. Joe showed the letter to Annand, who refused to read it.

"I decline to be a party to treasonable negotiations."

"Treasonable? If we refuse to negotiate, it will be clear that we have ignored the Queen's instructions to try for agreement. A very large sum of money may also be lost to Nova Scotia."

Annand's face looked pinched and pale and Joe wondered if he were ill. He knew Will, when he was under strain, suffered from bilious attacks.

"All negotiations of this kind," Annand said coldly, "ought to be conducted directly with me and my government, not with an individual." So this was where the shoe pinched!

"Come now, Will. You know Sir John wrote me because I have been the acknowledged leader of the anti-Confederates for two years – and also because you refused to even speak to him when he was here. You say the letter is treasonable." He offered it again. "You might at least read it." But again Annand brushed it aside.

"Have they offered you office yet?" he asked suddenly.

Joe nodded. "Well, yes, as a matter of fact –"

"I knew it," the other cut in triumphantly, "and in return you've promised to keep Nova Scotia quiet!"

"Naturally I refused it." He saw the red colour die out of Annand's face and was deeply sorry for him. "Did you really think I could bother about my own interests while we're still bargaining?"

"I suppose not," the other said with an effort. "All the same, I want nothing to do with any negotiations."

Joe made one last try. "Suppose I lock this letter up for six months, giving you time to try resolutions, delegations, anything else that's legal – what line will you take if you fail?"

There was this time no hesitation. "I'll go for annexation to the United States."

"Then we might as well part now," Joe said heavily. Annand made no further comment, but turned and walked out of the room.

Nearly a year was consumed in negotiations, with letters passing back and forth regularly between Halifax and the capital of Canada. Joe's partner in the struggle for better terms was a lumber-merchant and shipbuilder named Archibald McLelan. He was Liberal member for Colchester and the son of one of Howe's oldest friends. The two men had a difficult job. They had to bargain with the Canadians, using as their only strong card the danger of revolt or annexation, while at the same time they had to discourage the extremists in Nova Scotia who advocated such tactics. Macdonald wrote finally that everything was being done at his end to win the sympathy of the House to their case, and late in the year Howe and McLelan travelled to Portland, Maine, a convenient halfway point, to thrash out the last details with the Finance Minister.

In the end, they managed to wrest from Sir John Rose a credit of nearly a million dollars, money Nova Scotia could gradually spend for the benefit of her own people, as well as an annual payment of one hundred and sixty thousand dollars a year for ten years. Weary, reasonably content, the two Nova Scotians went on to Ottawa with Sir John Rose to complete the formal arrangements.

"We have now done justice so far as we could in monetary matters," Macdonald said, "and are prepared to deal with Nova Scotia in all other branches of the public service as rapidly as we get the power. But, Howe, we must have your help. I want you in my government, as a guarantee to give Parliament that when they have voted this money, the arrangement will not be repudiated by your province." He added, "The office of the Privy Council is open."

"I can't give you an answer at once," Howe told him, "but I will know for sure any day now." He was waiting for a reply from Gladstone in answer to the second application for Repeal. The reply came while he was still in Ottawa and was, as he had expected, a flat negative. Joe thereupon acknowledged the battle was over and his answer to Macdonald was "Yes." Though not anxious to continue in political life, there were no further *Albion* offers floating about and he must have money to live. Moreover, Macdonald's insistence that he participate in government coincided with his own determination to be where he could help the better terms motion through the House and where he could make sure that Nova Scotians got their fair share of jobs and honours in the new Dominion.

To save going home, then travelling back to be sworn in, Joe accepted the post there and then and was sworn in on the spot. To have gone home might have been wiser. He could then have told Nova Scotia face to face what he had done and why he had done it. As it was, the news of his appointment went ahead of him on the telegraph, coldly, without amplification. All Nova Scotia knew for nearly a week was that Howe had been given office—he had "accepted the situation."

The enemy, Annand and those who still held out against Confederation, leapt to take advantage of the situation.

"Howe has gone over to the enemy," they cried. "Howe has sold himself!"

And the news of better terms, when it came, could not compete with the shocking word—betrayal!

CHAPTER TWENTY
1869-1873

"The general answer I give to these slanders is simply my life."

Letter to Chronicle, 1869

There were only a few people at the station to meet him, and these few looked worried and spoke awkwardly. When he climbed into the carriage his son Will had brought, passers-by turned their heads instead of rushing to speak to him as they had always done. Driving home, he saw old friends turn down side streets to avoid him.

It was as if a darkness had fallen over Joe's town.

A few evenings later, he and Susan Ann went with another couple, probably the Stairs, to hear a band concert in the Public Gardens. We have a letter signed "L.S." describing what occurred: "It was a lovely evening and the Gardens were crowded, so much so we found it hard to walk through the paths. The illuminations were perfect, indeed everyone was seen as clearly as if in the light of day. My husband and Mrs. Howe were soon separated from us. Mr. Howe and I walked alone. As we passed, we heard on all sides our names in repeated undertones. Not one among the crowd spoke to Mr. Howe, no one seemed to even know him, who was head and shoulders above them all. It was some time before we met Mrs. Howe and my husband. She was very much excited and proposed that we go home. Mr. Howe and I did not exchange one word on our way. It does not take long to inflict a mortal wound, and that he had just received."

The love of the people had always been Joe's compensation for lack of material rewards. Now this too was refused him.

In order to take office, he had to be elected in Hants County, Nova Scotia. Since most of his constituents thought him a traitor, it would not be an agreeable contest. Yet it never occurred to him to draw back.

The previous year's campaign, a cheerful one run in company with friends before a friendly electorate, had been in fine weather. This year he would be travelling in winter, almost alone, with enemies on all sides. He was sixty-four, subject to heavy colds and bronchitis. Yet to all appearances, he set out as if to a picnic, the challenge appearing to act on him like a tonic.

Tupper had offered to "go around the course" with him and help, but Joe would have none of that. He would get elected by himself or not at all. He chose a young newsman, George Johnson, to go with him and edit an election fly-sheet. Johnson's paper, the *Reporter*, though not always on his side in politics, had never abused him personally. George, who could remember being taken as a small boy to hear the great Mr. Howe speak, had never really got over his hero worship. He turned out to be a good friend to Howe and an excellent eye witness and recorder of that frightful contest.

A man named Goudge, a clothing merchant of Halifax, was Joe's opponent. Annand, Wilkins, and two others accompanied Goudge and all made good use of the "Howe has sold his country" line. They had money left over from the Appeal Fund and spent it to buy "clacquers" as they were called, and put them in the crowd to lead the people in cat-calls. Joe had hard work sometimes even to make himself heard. "Annand has screamed repeal for nine months and has achieved nothing. Mr. McLelan and I—"

Yells of "turncoat" and "traitor" drowned his voice. He waited patiently, then started again. "Mr. McLelan and I have at all events got something to show for our labour, having rescued our people from direct taxation and received £40,000 to keep up our roads and bridges." The people stared up at him, silent for the moment, but angry with the one they had loved.

In spite of everything, he won converts here and there, but at a price. He had caught a cold at the start and had no chance to rest up. "The hard part," he told Sir John A. later, "was to make three speeches in a cold barn of a court house and to sit for hours in an atmosphere but a few degrees warmer than that of the street. Then when the meeting was over, my room at the hotel was filled till midnight with friends, organizing and consulting, from whom I could not escape. This sort of thing went on for fifteen days."

He had to ride through driving winds, sometimes snow, to the next meeting, then sit again for hours in wet clothing until it was his turn to speak. Often every breath seemed to cut his throat. "The day before I broke down, the meeting was held at Welsford in a drill shed with a ground floor, no fire and doors opening at both ends and which were hardly ever closed." His back had grown so painful, Johnson tried to get the meeting postponed, but the other side wouldn't hear of it. Howe himself insisted on going. "Can't afford to miss one meeting, George," he croaked, "I mustn't only win, but win with a majority big enough to show that better terms are acceptable to the people."

After he had sat in his chair for nearly two hours listening to Goudge and his running mate, he could endure the pain no longer. Wrapping himself in borrowed overcoats, he lay down at the back of the platform. It must have seemed to the audience – good hearted farmers most of them, who had known him for over thirty years – that his opponents were trampling on his prostrate form. When he rose to speak, he read the sympathy in their faces and his speaker's instinct responded. By sheer determination he forgot the pain and, transformed from a sick old man to a god with fiery eyes, he soon had the crowd in the hollow of his hand.

He remembered it was Susan Ann's birthday and sent her a message – "Your birthday has been a lucky day for me in all the concerns of life. May God spare you to see more of them, for I would rather lose a dozen elections than lose the smile which has cheered my wayward life." He told her not to fear that he would lose the election. "The game is ours, but we will work on to the end."

The next day, at Windsor, he was the last to arrive. The people, if they had looked carefully, would have seen that he was looking very old, his face even paler than usual. He had to force his way through the crowd to the platform and all the way there were voices hissing and shouting in his ear – "Traitor! Betrayer!" The meeting was in the Court House and there was a gallery, full this time of Goudge's clacquers who jeered and groaned as they got the signal from their leader.

In his opening speech, Joe tried to explain his reasons for opposing Confederation and why he had later decided he must accept the situation. "While there was a rational hope of obtaining a repeal of the B.N.A. Act, I struggled for two years to repeal it but I cannot work miracles, and am not such a fool as to deceive my countrymen, or pretend that I can. With infinite sorrow and mortification at the vain result of all our labours, I bow to the will of Providence."

He spoke his whole hour without a word or smile of encouragement and sat down without the clapping of a hand. It was Goudge's turn next and when he rose, the crowd, led by the clacquers, burst out in loud and long applause. When he finished, he was applauded again, and so was his running mate, Jones.

There was doubt at this point as to who should speak next. Some called for Annand, others for Howe to reply. After a few moments of this, Joe stood up and said with a smile that he would rather Mr. Annand would go on. Then he could take the whole batch of them together afterwards. "There was something wonderfully reassuring in this cheery remark," Johnson writes, "I thought the old man must surely be crushed, but here he was as cheerful and confident as ever." Annand said he would waive his right, as the hour was late.

So Howe got to his feet. He stood there for a moment, silent. Then, without any of his usual opening jokes, he spoke gravely:

"I cannot lie to you," he said. "I cannot amuse you with vain delusions. I do not believe in committing a body of honourable and loyal men to treason and insurrection without the smallest chance of success." Someone had just gone about lighting the lamps, and the face of the speaker was warmed by their glow. "For some old friends, misled by artful tales and persistent defamation, I feel a respect which cannot be impaired by one honest difference of opinion. They think me wrong and have acted upon the belief. I know I am right, and however high a value I set upon their personal regard, I cannot sacrifice to friends the interest of our country."

Slowly he gained and held their attention. "The parrot cry of all these others has been that Howe has sold the country, and this has been caught up by the newspapers controlled by Martin Wilkins and William Annand. The general answer I give to these slanders is simply my life, a life passed in your midst, in the open face of day, under the eye and observation, not only of the public men of our country, but of the great body of the people." In the gallery the clacquers started to drown Howe out and a man in the crowd turned on them – "Be quiet!" Someone clapped approvingly.

"When I left Nova Scotia in 1859, every pound that I could call my own had been earned before I accepted office. From that period to this day, I never bought an acre of land for myself or invested a pound for my family. Whoever heard of me trafficking in coal mines or gold mines or timber lands? Who ever heard of my profiting by the information I possessed when duties were to be raised or tariffs reconstructed? This is my answer to –" applause came then and was taken up and continued all over the room. He had to wait a full minute before going on. "This is my answer to the miserable pack who assail me, an answer you know to be accurate and indestructible. It is the answer every honest man in Nova Scotia can give and, on a moment's reflection will give, to the creatures who would sully the reputation of an old friend."

There was another burst of applause. "But who are these pure and disinterested patriots to whom money is no object and who are stirred with pious horror at the thought that I might have been influenced by mercenary considerations? I run my eye over the group," he turned and did so, "and will venture to say that a more corrupt pack cannot be found within the limits of the Dominion."

Feet began to stamp and there were shouts of approval and encouragement. Joe raised his hand and in an instant all was still.

From then on, they listened with bated breath, every so often breaking into laughter as he shook a wrathful finger at the two candidates and, as he said later, "wiped out their slates." Even the clacquers got carried away, ignored Goudge's signals and joined in the cheering.

When he finished, his voice was harsh and slow, but still compelling. After a short emotional pause, the crowd seemed to rise as one, swelling out the sides of the building in one great bellow of love and approval. Many who had whispered and hissed when he came in, came up afterwards to shake his hand and assure him of their votes.

Those nearest Joe, however, noted the deathly pallor of his face and saw him sway as he stepped down from the platform. Joe himself noticed that his heart was thumping and his legs felt like rubber. As a red mist gathered in front of his eyes, he reached out blindly for support. Hands grasped and held them, and he felt himself half-carried, half-led, through the crowd to the door. The cheering faded to a murmuring hush, and that was all he remembered until he awoke in bed in the hotel, with the doctor bending over him. He was kept in bed for most of a month and did no more electioneering then, or thereafter.

Yet he won.

Fifteen hundred and twelve votes to Goudge's eleven hundred and twenty-nine gave Joe the clear majority he wanted. "Election now secure," he telegraphed his friend, Governor Doyle. "League and locals licked to sticks."

But he had paid dearly for his triumph. Physically, he would never again be the same Joe Howe.

The election was in February and March. In May, Joe and his wife went to Ottawa and Howe entered the Macdonald Cabinet. "We had hard work pushing our extra subsidies through," he wrote Governor Doyle. "Had our men remained at home as they were advised, and had I not gone into the Cabinet, there would not have been a ghost of a chance of getting one dollar awarded." He made sure Dominion patronage was fairly dealt out to his province. "Hardly a week passes," he wrote, "that I have not the opportunity to protect or promote the interest of some Nova Scotian at home or abroad, and the days are marked with white chalk when this can be done."

He held no grudges. He secured, for instance, a Supreme Court judgeship for Jonathon McCully, the man who more than any other, perhaps, had tied his hands in the battle against union. He replied to McCully's rather awkward letter of thanks: "It was not possible to pass you over, as there could be no question as to fitness and qualifications. Our modern differences of opinion on the question of Confederation were left out of view, since the policy (whether right or wrong) had been accepted and the experiment was to be fairly tried. Personal feelings I had none to indulge, as we had a good deal that was pleasant to remember, and whatever there was of an opposite character, it was my duty to forget."

Once in the Cabinet, it was the job he thought of first, and it was not in him to do any job half-heartedly. When Macdonald made him Secretary of State for the Provinces, he resolved at once to visit the Red River and see the new province of Manitoba for himself. To get there, he had to travel by train through the States to rail's end at St. Cloud, then ride and walk with a party of young men for another twenty-two days, mostly through heavy rain. He was sixty-five years old and suffered a good deal from pain in his chest, yet he enjoyed the outgoing journey. He was in many respects the same man who long ago had walked gaily and inquisitively through the Nova Scotian woods. His insatiable curiosity took him one day miles out of his way just to visit a famous cave, and another time to view a waterfall. He wrote home a merry account of taking part in dances and songs around the campfire at night. At one place they heard there was trouble ahead. The Métis, under Louis Riel, had sent word that the new Governor,

William McDougall, was not to be allowed in the country. Howe's group decided to go on just the same and there were no obstructions.

Arriving at Fort Garry at last, Joe was received with rough hospitality and told that Riel had left to stop the Governor at the border. Though an official of government, there was nothing Howe could do about it. The main thing was to show no favouritism to either side. He allayed their fears as well as he could. During his brief stay, he met and talked with most of the leading men of the new province and is described by one writer of the day as "a kindly, old-fashioned gentleman," not exactly a picture of the Howe who, less than a year before, had slashed at his enemies from a score of election platforms in Hants County.

He made notes for his report to the Prime Minister on Canada's newest province. The English were uneasy because they had not been consulted in the transfer of their colony, a view with which he could sympathize. On the other hand, he understood the fears of the Métis who saw in McDougall another hard-hearted Scot like those who had so long ruled them in the Hudson's Bay Company and who might allow the English to lord it over them and deprive them of their language and religion.

When he left the Red River, the country was peaceful. All was well except that winter had begun to show its cold and snowy face across the prairie. The journey back must have been a nightmare. Joe slogged with his party through wet snow all day, beating against a wind always in his face, and slept fitfully at night with the pain of swollen legs, under dripping canvas. Arrived back at last in Ottawa, he was just in time to take his seat in the House and had no time to rest. There McDougall accused him of stirring up insurrection in the Red River colony, and Joe replied hotly, offering to produce witnesses to prove that his behaviour had been proper at all times. The Prime Minister assured him that it was unnecessary and the House too supported him against McDougall, who was known to be difficult. "He went asking for trouble," John A. told Howe. "Of course the people of the colony are not blameless either. The Métis must understand that the country has been bought by Canada and must be ruled by Canada, by force if necessary." Howe disagreed with the Prime Minister about using force, claiming it would be better to abandon the province altogether if it could not be ruled by fair and considerate means. "Let the grass grow over the prairie and the wild animals roam the woods again," cried the son of Sandemanian John Howe, "but let us not go hence to shed human blood."

Macdonald smiled at the foolish idealism of an old man and went his way. The Riel Rebellion was the result, and his government's mistaken policy created a racial resentment felt to this day.

Thankfully, when the Session was finally over, Joe and his wife went to Philadelphia where he enjoyed a rest and medical treatment. They were there all winter and from that vantage point Joe watched with growing dismay the progress of Canadian negotiations with the United States over certain matters in dispute between them. Macdonald, the representative of Canada, worked hard in the face of conflicting British wants and did far better then he had expected, but the treaty which grew out of the meeting certainly sacrificed Canadian interests. Joe was furious at the concessions, particularly those which affected Nova Scotian fisheries.

In a speech he made to the Ottawa Young Men's Christian Association in 1872, he said that if Englishmen were determined to abandon Canada, Canadians had the nerve and ability to work out their own destiny alone. It was perhaps the closest he ever came to publicly casting off his allegiance to Britain. It is plain, too, that he was starting to think in a Canadian way as well as a Nova Scotian one, for we find him writing in this spirit to a friend on the Pacific coast: "Your letter of the third of May is beside me and it is pleasant to hear from a friend who overlooks the Pacific and to feel that we are interested in the same objects and are citizens of the same country." Given more time, Joe Howe might have lived in history not only as a devoted Nova Scotian but as a staunch Canadian.

Macdonald, however, was not happy about the publicity given Howe's speech and trembled for international peace. "He must go," he said aloud one day in his office, and a secretary hastened to agree. "A foolish old man," the secretary said, "and a great trouble-maker."

Now Macdonald had often spoken angrily of Howe, referring to him as "that pestilent fellow" in the days of the Confederation battle, but his judgment was in general fair and so he now shook his head. "No, not a trouble-maker, and certainly not foolish. There are, and always have been, more seminal ideas in that man's head, all of them important, than in any other man's with whose history I am familiar. We must find him something honourable and worthy of his reputation."

Outspokenness had often got Joe into trouble, but now, for once, it brought him reward. He was invited to become Nova Scotia's next Lieutenant-Governor. Strange, thought Joe sadly, that honour and place should come to him at last, not from long-loved and well-served Britain, but from upstart Canada.

The trouble was, it had come rather late.

"General Doyle's term of service as Governor expires in May," Joe wrote Admiral Westphal, his wife's uncle in the Isle of Wight, "and my colleagues have offered me the place which, if I live, I intend to accept – first, because it makes an adequate provision for my family for five years, which is as long a period as I shall care to remain in the public service; secondly, because it crowns my long and trying public life with the highest position open to me in my native province; and thirdly, because it takes us home to spend the evening of our days among those who are most near and dear to us."

He assured the Admiral that Susan Ann was enjoying good health. "I send you a number of the *Canadian Monthly* in which you will find some verses addressed to her, written many years ago but which have only just been published. After forty years' further experience of her many virtues, I believe the portraiture to be as faithful now as it was in 1832. You will be gratified to know that my own constituency, in the midst of whom I had to fight so hard a battle four years ago, this summer re-elected me by acclamation without my ever spending a shilling or even being in the country."

He heard from Governor Doyle that there was a small amount of opposition to him still in Nova Scotia and he warned Howe not to show official discrimination when he came to Government House. "Have no fear," Joe replied, "I have not been accustomed to treat people who are courteous and civil with rudeness or unfairness, and it is too late for me to begin now."

His Ottawa colleagues gave him a rousing send-off at the station, but for once he had not the energy to answer with more than an emotional word of thanks. The journey further exhausted him and when he arrived in Halifax, he looked old and feeble, not the Joe Howe the people remembered. There was a large crowd this time, to greet the new Governor, but seeing him, their cheers died. After a few friends had gone up and spoken to him, the others stood back, not wanting to delay his ride to Government House where he could rest. Yet a few days later, when he took his oath of office, he stood tall and spoke in a firm voice, and they thought perhaps now he was home his health would quickly mend. Joe himself assured them that it would.

Of course he was visited by the press. One man came who was from Johnson's paper and it may have been Johnson himself. Whoever he was, he found the Governor upstairs in his old dressing-gown, writing at his desk. "But I don't mind you," said his Excellency cheerfully. "You're a newspaperman and know how much easier it is to write with everything loose about you. Come in, my dear chap." They talked of newspaper work and of the recent toll of death in the wreck of the steamship *Atlantic* just off Halifax Harbour, which led them to speak of the great question of what came after death. "Fear of death is natural to man," Howe said thoughtfully, "as is the fear of an old woman to enter for the first time a railway car, but if the right view is taken, death should not be dreaded, rather welcomed. The grub shivers and trembles but its death is development. The gay golden-winged butterfly springs into existence."

From his bedroom window, Joe could look across the road and see the old graveyard where his parents lay buried. He thought how pleased old John Howe would have been to see his beloved son in this place. He remembered his predecessors, Kempt and Campbell and Falkland, and smiled. A pretty good life he'd had on the whole. He wished his financial position were brighter, for the sake of Susan Ann and the boys. He must live as long as he could, if only to earn sufficient for their needs after he was gone. If he died now, he would be leaving only the house on Granville Street, some furniture, less than a thousand dollars in the bank. He would like to live, anyway, to find out what kind of shot he made at being Governor.

Yet he sensed that his time was growing short. He suffered almost continuously with pain in his chest.

On the night of Saturday, May 31, 1873 – only three weeks after coming to Government House – Joe walked the study floor in torment during most of the night. Around half-past four, Susan Ann suggested he go to his bed. "The change might help. Perhaps you could even sleep." When he agreed to try, she and their son Will supported him on either side as he began the slow walk to his bedroom. Before he reached it, he began to sink in their grasp, a dead weight, as if his strength had suddenly gone.

"Can you reach the chair?" his wife asked anxiously.

"I don't think so."

They let him sink down on the carpet then, with his head and shoulders resting on his wife's lap. He talked to them for a while, his voice strong still, his hand firm and his mind clear to the last moment. When release came, they could only be thankful his sufferings were over. The verdict of the doctors at that time was "lung congestion." One of today's leading heart specialists says the account of his illness and death shows all the classic symptoms of *myocardial infarction*, or heart disease.

The next morning, Sunday, in St. Paul's during the service, a man came up the aisle and handed a note to the rector. He read it, then after a longish pause, said very slowly: "I regret to announce that Lieutenant-Governor Howe has just passed

215

away." There was no sound from a congregation suddenly struck dumb. Then, the rector dismissing them, they got up and worked their way out, men and women alike struggling to hide their tears.

Slowly, all over the province, the news spread.

"Howe is dead."

In small villages, in towns, in the remotest parts of the province, farmers, fishermen, tradesmen, housewives, merchants, children, and beggars, all were struck speechless. They stood where they had been standing when they first heard, tools in hand, jobs forgotten, trying to grasp it. Howe dead? Somehow they had believed he would never die. He had always been with them, a part of their lives.

Loneliness swept over them then, and they wept for their loss.

The funeral was impressive. All the important people were there. Was Annand? Probably. How would he feel? Had he ever made up with his old friend? Nearly everyone had. A few must have walked in that procession bitterly sorry they had refused his generous hand.

Flags flew at half-mast. City, town and country grieved not for a lieutenant-governor, but as if they were all one household mourning the loss of a father.

Amongst the thousands of sympathy letters was one from the son of Herbert Huntington. "The pain that I at first felt on hearing the sad announcement," he wrote Syd Howe, "has been succeeded by a feeling of utter 'ir-reconcilement' to coin a word for the occasion. I will not say how I felt or what I did when the tidings reached me, but I will repeat what my friend and your father's friend, John Hatfield, said: 'I had a good cry for half an hour after.'"

The Halifax *Evening Express*, a few short years back one of Howe's harshest critics, wrote: "We need hardly speak of the regrets of those who, during so many years, have been aided by him, who never aided him very much, who have lived in positions in which he placed them and had a quietude in the public service which he never had, till it came to him at last, the quietude of the grave."

Why is it this man, so well loved in his day, is still remembered? He was a failure in the eyes of many. He made no fortune, gained few honours. He was frustrated in his great plan for the federation of the Empire, and he failed to stop Confederation. True, he led and won the battle for responsible government, a revolution as complete as any ever fought, and won it without a shot being fired; true, he kept the peace in Nova Scotia at a dangerous moment in her history. But is it for these things he's remembered? Or is it because, for all his human frailties, he was one of the last of the true heroes, a statesman who consciously, deliberately and with consistency put his country and his countrymen ahead of his own interests.

In his day, men bragged if they had once held Joe Howe's horse. Children boasted if Mr. Howe had kissed them or held them on his knee. And as recently as last year, a lady in Hantsport, moving from her old home to another, insisted on taking her front door boot-scraper with her, because Joe Howe had once scraped his boots on it.

George Johnson writes that some years after Howe's death, he visited Camp Hill cemetery to look at his grave, marked by a modest shaft of grey Nova Scotian granite. "All other graves," Johnson said, "have green grass in front of them, but his is trodden down to brown earth by the multitudes who stop to look upon the last resting place of our greatest Nova Scotian."

As one newsman of his day put it: "He made Nova Scotia from his dreams of her."

He *was* Nova Scotia.

Suggestions for Further Reading

Akins, Thomas B. "History of Halifax City." *Morning Herald*, 1895. Reprinted by Mika Publishing, Belleville, 1973.

Annand, William. *The Speeches and Public Letters of Joseph Howe*. Boston: John P. Jewett and Co., 1858.

Beck, James Murray. *Joseph Howe: Voice of Nova Scotia*. Toronto: McClelland and Stewart Ltd., 1964.

————. *Joseph Howe, Anti-Confederate*. Ottawa: Canadian Historical Association Booklet, 1965.

————. "A Fool for a Client." *Acadiensis* (Halifax), Vol. 3, No. 2 (Spring 1974).

Burroughs, Peter. *The Colonial Reformers and Canada*. Toronto: McClelland and Stewart Ltd., 1969.

Campbell, Duncan. *History of Nova Scotia*. Montreal: John Lovell, 1873.

Chisholm, Joseph A. *The Speeches and Public Letters of Joseph Howe*. 2 vols. Halifax: Halifax *Chronicle*, 1909.

Craig, Gerald M. (ed.) *Lord Durham's Report*. Toronto: McClelland and Stewart Ltd., 1963.

Elliott, Shirley B. *A History of Province House*. Halifax: The Queen's Printer, 1979.

Grant, George Munro. *Joseph Howe*. Halifax: A. and W. Mackinlay, 1904.

Harvey, Daniel Cobb. *The Heart of Howe*. Toronto: Oxford University Press, 1939.

Howe, Joseph. *Howe Papers 1870-1873*. Ottawa: Public Archives of Canada.

Johnson, George. "Biography of Joseph Howe." Unpublished. Ottawa: Public Archives of Canada.

Lynch, Peter. "Early Reminiscences of Halifax." *Nova Scotia Historical Society*, Vols. 16 and 17.

Martin, Chester. *Empire and Commonwealth*. Toronto: Oxford University Press, 1929.

Martell, James S. *Government House*. Halifax: Public Archives of Nova Scotia, Vol. 1, No. 4.

Morison, Gene. *The Brandy Election 1830*. Halifax: Nova Scotia Historical Society, Vol. 30 (1954).

Parks, M.G. (ed.) *Joseph Howe; Western and Eastern Rambles: Travel Sketches of Nova Scotia*. Toronto: University of Toronto Press: 1973.

————. (ed.) *Poems and Essays of Joseph Howe*. Toronto: University of Toronto Press, 1973.

Patterson, George G. *Studies in Nova Scotia History*. Halifax: Imperial Publishing Co., 1940.

Percy, H.R. *Joseph Howe*. Toronto: Fitzhenry and Whiteside, 1976.

Punch, Terence. "The Halifax Connection 1749-1848: A Century of Oligarchy in Nova Scotia." Unpublished Ph.D. dissertation. Halifax: Provincial Archives of Nova Scotia, 1973.

Stayner, Charles. "The Sandemanian Loyalists." Halifax: Nova Scotia Historical Society, Vol. 29 (1951).

Story, Norah. *The Church and State Party in Nova Scotia 1749-1851*. Halifax: Nova Scotia Historical Society, Vol. 27 (1947).

Waite, Peter B. *The Life and Times of Confederation*. Toronto: Oxford University Press, 1962.

Acknowledgements

I must first thank the Canada Council's Canadian Horizons Program, for without its assistance this book could not have been attempted.

The greater part of my research was done at the Public Archives of Nova Scotia, whose staff led me cheerfully and patiently through the mass of Howe material. Dr. Phyllis Blakeley, Associate Archivist, gave me additional time and attention, and read the manuscript. Dr. Murray Beck, Howe's most comprehensive biographer, explained several political puzzles for me and, if I have still got things wrong, it is not his fault.

I must not forget either to thank the Rt. Rev. Monseigneur Gerald P. Murphy of Ketch Harbour for allowing me, during the years of work on Howe's life, to wear out his two valuable volumes of Chisholm's *Speeches and Letters of Joseph Howe*.

Ketch Harbour, N.S.